2 in *1* in 2

The Supreme *Revelation*

ISBN: 978-0-9892826-6-6

LWUM

Learn with universal mind publishing

Sacred texts decoded

A Gathering Trumpet for an

Enlightened Kingdom

on Earth

This was narrated by X.H. New Wisdom, the brother of the twin; the sister, Helen Xinhui Zhu, wrote it down.

This writing was not touched by another human hand during the writing process, so please forgive for any editing mistakes.

Foreword

Those who read and believe are blessed to rise, those who believe and bring these to others are blessed to rise and live in Love and happiness in Kingdom forever; those who hear and believe are awakened; those who hear but refuse to believe sleep forever in future generations

I am the beginning and the dissolution of everything and everything emanates from Me. Without my energy, no living entities can live in either spiritual or material world

Whenever there is a decline in true religious practice, and a predominant rise of irreligion - at that time I descend Myself, to deliver the pious and to annihilate the miscreants, as well as to reestablish the principles of religion, I Myself appear, millennium after millennium

The principle of True Religion is the Eternal Love of the Eternal Family

I am sending my Spirit to the world to lift you, some do not recognize Herim*[1] because SHe*[2]is disguised in same dresses as you do; some feel jealous of Herim because they want to be like Herim; some feel unease because Heris*[3] words lash your souls; However many of you love Herim

---

[1] [hᵊrim]

[2] [(shᵊ'hi)]

[3] [hᵊriz]

and take Heris words, for these you are blessed people

- God, the Supreme Spirit, the Supreme Personality
  of God Head, Tao, Allah

The world is changing

I feel it in the water, I smell it in the air,

I see it everywhere

I wish it in my heart, I am in it...

Part I

The Three Tier Messages

CONTENTS

Beginning

One in Two, Two in One, Evolving Forever

The Taichi Yin Yang Symbol encodes the secret of secrets that God wants to deliver to humankind through a process of consciousness evolution

Before you continue, close your eyes and take 3 deep slow breaths, let your attention focus on your breaths, one…….two……..three…….. Now open your eyes and look at the Yin-Yang symbol on next page consciously:

Fig. 1#

What do you see?

The other night, I had a dream: *I was standing on the earth, a few planets, rotating, were slowly moving in front of me in the space sky, like a movie. A glowing, illusive ball, looked like the Taichi Yin-Yang ball appeared in the sky. In the glowing ball the white and the black parts were in transparence, not very distinguishable from each other, then a lot of hands came out of it, with their palms stretched.*

Though I did not quite understand the meaning, I felt very uplifted and pulled to doing some research and meditation on the Taichi symbol.

When staring into the picture, my sight first caught the black shadow, by focusing on the white dot in the black shadow while being aware of the white part, the white part starts to expand fully to covering the black shadow and merging with the small white dot, so the whole picture becomes a white ball with just the small black dot in it; then I changed my attention to the white part, focusing on the black dot while being aware of the black shadow, the black shadow starts to expand to fully covering the white part and merging with the small black dot, so the whole picture becomes a black ball just with the small white dot in it.

The Messages: One in Two, Two in One, evolving forever come to me in meanings of 3 tiers

Every existence, from the macro cosmos to micro subatomic particles; from the galaxies, stars to human beings, animals to the cells of any living organisms; from energy to matter, the entire universe is a One whole piece which but comprises two main opposite forces – the forward driving Yang force and the still holding Yin force. Each of the two opposite forces forever strives to surpass the other, within the **Law of Balance** which is the invisible One that withholds the two eternal dancers. And with this eternal dance, life is generated, propelled and evolved in cycle. If we see the invisible One, the Law of Balance as the circle enclosing the Black and White parts in the Yin-Yang symbol, we would understand that at one particular point or one particular moment the black and white parts are not equal nor same to each other in the circle, but as a whole One 3-dimensional object it is a balanced ball. Similarly in the universe, at one point the Yin – Yang forces do not necessarily equal to each other, but in a multi-dimensional space-time the whole One system is held in balance, which is governed by the Oneness Consciousness that is in constant motion. The Yin and Yang forces represent different elements in different life forms, and in different stage of the same life form at different space time, therefore do not permanently refer to the same things. In other words, in reality the 'circle' or the 'ball' is not necessarily perfectly round, but as a whole it is a balanced one in which all elements exist in relative harmony to achieve its manifesting state.

万物复阴而抱阳，冲气以为和。All things carry on the back female and embrace male, wrestling each other in Spirit they reach harmony

-   *Laozi, Tao Te Jing*

Chapter 1

Message Tier No.1

The universe evolves in the dance of Law of Evolution and Law of Gravitation within the Law of Balance

In astronomy, a star is understood as a massive, luminous sphere of gas held by its own gravity and its life processing inner motion plus other forces in its surrounding environment in the interstellar space. A star is born from the gravitational attraction amidst an interstellar cloud – Nebula of dusts, hydrogen, helium and other gases which are produced and released from a previous life cycle: these elements are sent into motion from the explosion of previous stars, and gradually a stellar core is formed. At the beginning life of a star, with the contraction of the gravity the stellar core becomes sufficiently dense to a point of 18 million Fahrenheit degrees, a transformation happens: the hydrogen becomes steadily converted into helium through nuclear fusion, releasing energy into its outer space in the process, through which the internal pressure is generated to counter-effect its own gravitation and to prevent it from contracting further to reach a balance, then the star would enter its relatively stable stage of life for billions of years. The nuclear fusion makes the star shine. Once the hydrogen fuel at the core is exhausted, a star with at least 0.4 times the mass of the Sun expands to become a red giant, in some cases fusing heavier elements at the core or in shells around the core. The star then evolves into a degenerate form, recycling a portion of its matter into the interstellar environment, where it will contribute to the formation of a new generation of stars. Meanwhile, the core becomes a stellar remnant: a white dwarf or a neutron star which still produces energy and cloud dusts that may be also part of the roles in the formation of a new generation of stars.

In a star's life, if we see its gravity that tries to hold everything back towards its core as the Yin force, and the nuclear fusion that sets everything apart from its core as the Yang force which is the urge for new life generation propelled by the Law of Evolution, then at some point these two forces have to reach a balance to keep the star at a stable state for its life sustaining process. If on one hand its gravity, the Yin force is more than the pressure released by the nuclear fusion plus other outer forces, then the star would contract further (would not be a star), and on the other hand if the nuclear fusion plus other outer forces is more than the gravity force, then the mass of the star would be blown away from its core. Therefore the Law of Balance plays an important role in a star's life. This Law of Balance may involve a lot of forces from both within and without the star, especially from the interstellar space.

While in a star's life cycle, from before the point of reaching nuclear fusion, through the relatively stable state of nuclear fusion, to expanding to a red giant, to a heavy white dwarf, a low mass black dwarf, the gravity force and the evolution force overcomes each other, the Yin Yang forces break their balance at a specific point, causing the star evolve to the next stage of its life.

The Law of Balance is the most intricate law in a galaxy to keep an orderly system of new-born stars, red-giants, white dwarfs, black dwarfs, neutron stars or black holes, and it has the same effects in the entire universe to keep an orderly system of galaxies and all other known and unknown elements in the entire space. Under this mysterious and opulent Divine order, new stars, galaxies, and larger systems are born, life forms are generated and evolves in the cosmic domain.

With these three main laws, the infinite cosmos evolves forever, humankind will continue to be astonished that the universe (it is given the name as universe, but you truly mean the whole existing environment where humankind lives) as a whole has no boundary and expands inwardly and outwardly without limit - new smaller subatomic elements will be discovered, and new bigger systems more than galaxies, visible universe will be discovered. Wherever the awareness of humankind reaches, new wonders will be realized. Therefore 'cosmos' is really the word for the existing environment where all beings dwell in.

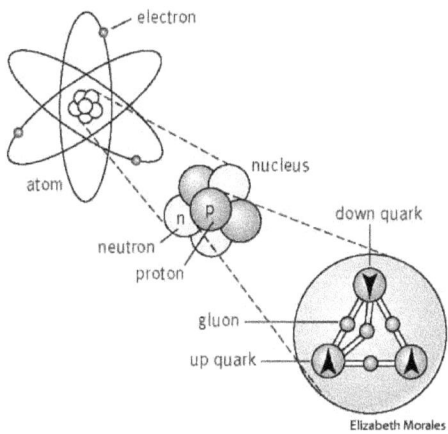

electron

nucleus

atom

n p

neutron

proton

down quark

gluon

up quark

Elizabeth Morales

Fig.2#

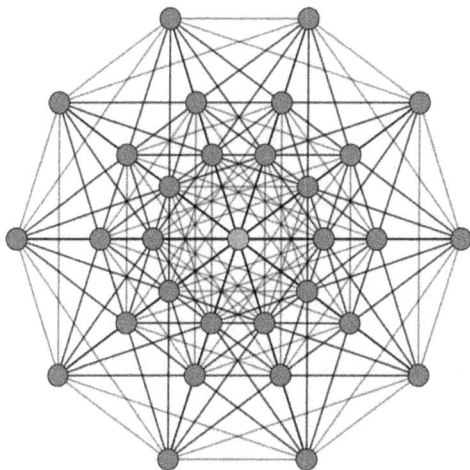

Fig.3# source from Tumruen

" ... There is no being, moving or nonmoving that can exist without Me. ... There is no end to My divine manifestations... Know that all opulent, beautiful and glorious creations spring from but a spark of My splendor... With a single fragment of Myself I pervade and support this entire universe"

- *The Personality of God Head, Bhagavad Gita 10.39-42*

"You are without origin, middle or end. Your glory is unlimited... Although You are one, You spread throughout the sky and the planets and all space between"

- *Arjuna, Bhagavad Gita 11.19-20*

The formation of the Taichi (Taiji) Yin-Yang Symbol itself reveals the evolution of human consciousness, and That in play is God Consciousness

Today's Taijitu, diagram of supreme ultimate, the Yin-Yang symbol which is universally used to represent the concept of change between Yin-Yang forces in the nature, has taken a long journey to come into its present image.

By observing the move of the sun, the moon and stars, the

ancient Chinese recorded the cycles of the day, the month, the year, the 4 seasons, 24 subseasons and they noticed the changes of Chi, the life force in the nature. By Han dynasty (202 BCE-220AD), the 24 seasons were adopted, and it was officially established in the calendar published in 104 BCE.

Below is the diagram for season changes of a year: by marking positions of the sun light (white) called Yang and dimmer moonlight (black) called Yin, it illustrated the Yin-Yang changes. Yang would not grow without Yin. Yin could not give birth without Yang. Yin is born (begins) at Summer Solstice and Yang is born (begins) at Winter Solstice - each of the two starts well within middle of the other.

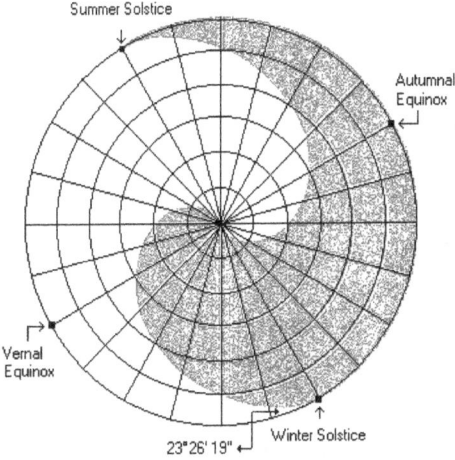

Fig 4# source from Allen Tsai

11

The Concepts of Wuji (Limitless, Infinite) and Taiji (Supreme Ultimate) first appeared in works of Taoist philosophies during the era of Spring-Autumn & Warring States (770-221 BCE) in the land called Middle Kingdom:

From *the book* **TaoTeJing,** which was attributed to Laozi who was believed to live about 130 years from around 600 to 470BCE,

"道生一，一生二，二生三，三生万物。"

"From Tao comes One, One Breeds Two, Two produces Three. Three gives birth to all things" （TTJ.42）

In verse 42 of TaoTeJing, although it did not mention the words 'Wuji' and 'Taiji', it is the earliest reference to the concepts of "Wuji" and "Taiji"

Here it is understood that Tao is Wuji, Infinity; One refers to Taiji, Supreme Ultimate; Two refers to Yin and Yang forces; and Three refers to the progenitors of all manifestations.

The understanding of the verse is like 'From Tao (the Law of Nature or the Law of Heaven, Infinity) comes One (the Supreme Ultimate, infinite); One (the Supreme Ultimate) breeds Two (the Yin-Yang forces), the Two Yin-Yang forces working as One produce three progenitors, which are the Two-in-One God, the three progenitors give birth to all things.

This verse also reveals the non-dual and duality concepts with reference to One and Two concepts. In the following verse 'Wuji, Infinite' is directly mentioned:

"知其白守其黑，为天下式。为天下式，常德不忒，复归于无极。"

"Know whiteness (Yang) while maintaining blackness(Yin), and be a model for all under heaven. By being a model for all under heaven, Eternal integrity (by holding Two in One) will not err. If Eternal integrity does not err, you will return to Infinity (Wuji) again"(TTJ. 28)

In later history, other Taoist philosophers, like Zhuangzi (369-286 BCE), several Taoist and rationalist philosophers in Song Dynasty (960-1279AD) who had been influenced by Laozi, explained and developed the concepts.

While the earliest Taijitu, Diagram of Supreme Ultimate can be traced to I-Jing, the Book of Change, a classic Chinese book on divination according to the Yin-Yang changes in the nature, dated 1100-300 BCE.

By 1100 BCE in Zhou dynasty, there were only 8 seasons recognized. The Taijitu was obtained by drawing 8 divisions according to the 8 seasons. And it was developed and passed down through couple of master-disciple cycles in Song Dynasty, to a philosopher and cosmologist, Zhou Dun Yi周敦颐 (AD 1017–1073), in his book *Taijitu shuo* 太極圖說 (Explanation of the Diagram of the Supreme Ultimate) Zhou explained in details the concepts of Wuji, Taiji and the Yin Yang, and their relationships what he believed, with a diagram in it. And it is believed that the current Taijitu came from Zhou.

Fig5#

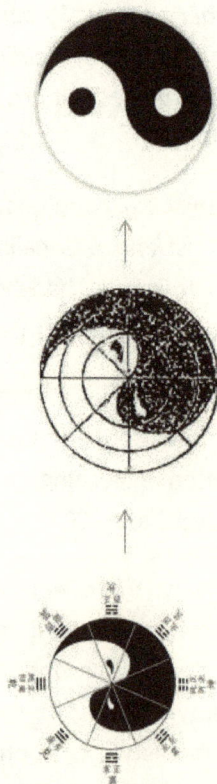

A Simple Illustration of the Development of the Taiji Symbol

The formation history of the Taiji symbol did not take place in one single short time, instead it took a long process through thousands of years, reflecting the progress of humankind's understanding about the nature and the expansion of their consciousness.

The most amazing and mysterious thing is that the one symbol originated in one single geographical location conveys so powerful and the same messages that are capsulated in the main concepts and beliefs about nature, beings, God, demigods and their relationships held in many ancient scripts in different cultures

The Taiji and Yin Yang (Two) forces are concepts of the dual reality in the manifested world, and Wuji, Infinity is the non-duality in the unmanifested reality.

In Geneses 1.27, the lines were written this way:

So God created humankind in his image,
in the image of God He created them;
male and female He created them.

Traditionally it is understood this is talking about the creation of a man and a woman. Wasn't it repetitive if the first 2 lines were talking about the same? Also we noticed in the lines, 'God' was capitalized in singularity while in chapter 1.26 'God' were plural – "Let us make humankind in our image, according to our likeness..." and in other places when talking about human creation 'Lord God' was used.

So the three lines of messages should be understood as:

Oneness God created humankind (as one) in his image of Oneness,

Oneness God created human beings (numerous) in his Oneness image;

Yang and Yin two forces God created in them

Throughout the scriptures there are places where man/male and woman/female were used as metaphors.

In Gospel of Thomas, verse 11, Jesus said: *"On the day when you were one you became two."*

This was referring that Adam and Eve without listening to God's warning, ate the fruit of the knowledge tree resulting in obtaining the ability to perceive 'good and evil' and shutting down the eternal life, therefore from non-duality slipped to duality

In verse 22, when His disciples asked when they would enter the Kingdom, Jesus said to them,

"*When you make the two one, ... and when you make the male and the female one and the same, so that the male not be male nor the female female; ... then will you enter [the Kingdom]."*

In Verses 7.4 -7.6, Bhagavad Gita, from one of Hindis ancient epics, the Supreme Personality of God Head said when revealing the nature of all beings:

"Earth, water, fire, air, ether, mind, intelligence and false ego - all together these eight constitute My separated material energies."

"Besides these,... there is another superior energy of Mine, which comprises the living entities who are exploiting the resources of this material, inferior nature"

"All created beings have their source in these two natures. Of all that is material and all that is spiritual in this world, know for certain that I am both the origin and the dissolution"

How could it be so coincident that in all major ancient scriptures originated from different culture geographies the messages of Oneness God with two opposite forces had been injected in all beings during their creation if it were not from a Supreme One Conscious Mind, that was waving His mighty 'hand' and writing the masterstrokes, whatever you may call it – God, Universal Mind, the Supreme Spirit etc.? How can it not be the work of Oneness God that the splendid and sophisticated manifestations of macro and micro cosmos keep blowing human's minds and dazzling their eyes with all those new wondrous discoveries?

Chapter 2

Message Tier No.2

At a planetary domain, the Earth is in the challenge of balancing the Yin-Yang forces. The law is taking its course, forcing the main player on the earth to adjust itself

One of the celestial bodies in the solar system is called Earth. This is the planet where human beings and some other God's creations inhabit.

The age of the Earth is about 4.54 billion years, similar to that of the Sun (4.567 billion years). The sun was formed from the gravitational contraction from a nebula dust cloud. At the moment the Sun was born, the sudden nuclear fusion burst from the center of the Sun repelled away its outer space dusts which were moving towards the Sun's center by its gravitation meanwhile sending extreme heat through radiation to its outer space dusts within the nebula cloud. These dusts gained momentum by the push and the heat from the Sun and started a process of sticky collision during which the dust particles steadily accumulate masses to form ever-larger bodies, and by the Sun's gravitation, they were attracted towards the Sun within its relatively cleared surroundings till the bodies became massive enough, plus other forces from the interstellar space, to prevent themselves further moving towards the Sun instead start to orbit it. One of the solar planetary objects was the Earth.

From space, the earth is seen as a globe with blue and white patterns orbiting the Sun in the Solar system. The earth is covered by over 70% ocean and the rest by continents. Above the earth's surface is a layer of gases, the atmosphere which mainly contains oxygen used by most organisms for respiration, nitrogen, and carbon dioxide used by plants, algae and other bacteria for photosynthesis. The atmosphere plays the role in regulating the surface temperatures and keeping the warms as well as protecting all living organism on Earth from genetic damage by solar ultraviolet radiation.

Unlike the Sun, the earth's mass is not big enough to have a gravity to contract its mass to a point where it can generate nuclear fusion to process its life. As a planet, the earth's life journey is to orbit the Sun. The earth's life span may be tied to that of the Sun if there is not an 'accident', say being hit by another massive enough object. Then to the earth, it does not matter if its orbit becomes closer to the sun or farther away from the Sun or keeps the same distance but change its rotating behaviors. In other words, the earth has different possibilities to evolve its life. It can be like Venus with its surface temperature at 462 °C (863 °F), or be like Mars with a temperature of big difference between 35 to -143°C (95 to -225.4 °F).

However all the life forms on the earth, which are both part of its life generating forces and subject to the outcomes of this life procession, will take the consequences without any options therefore it comes to the evolution of lives on Earth.

It is obvious for all lives on the earth to hope that the planet could maintain its 'good' relationship with its orbiting center, the Sun and not to have a drastic change on its overall conditions, the opposite of which would lead to an irrevocable impact on the future of the planet and of all lives on it.

The Yin-Yang forces on the planet have been in unbalance for a long time, the whole system is under challenge

If the earth's gravitation is viewed as the Yin force which is in constant motion trying to hold the earth toward its core to stabilize itself by offsetting all forces pulling it outward from its core; all the activities underneath and above its surface, and gravitational forces and other forces from other space objects, such as the Sun, the moon, other planets, space dusts etc. are seen together as the Yang force which propels the earth moving forward its life. Then there is a balance to be kept in order for the earth to keep an overall 'right' condition to sustain the current life forms on it while orbiting and rotating.

The earth by either losing or gaining mass enough may

alter its orbit, and a change in mass distribution on earth may cause its underneath pressure losing balance therefore induce earthquakes, volcanoes, landslides etc. which may further trigger other energy releasing activities such as shifting its axis. According to NASA, the 9.0 magnitude earthquake that ravaged Japan in 2011 shortened Earth's day by over one-millionth of a second, and it also shifted the Earth's axis by about 6.5 inches, which would definitely alter other forces for its life procession on Earth.

The Sun's mass takes 99.86% of the whole solar system and its size is roughly 1,000,000 times of the earth. Since it is so massive compared to the earth, its gravitation can be viewed as a stable factor in Earth's Yang force.

The rest of Yang force activities related to the earth are: geothermal acts in the earth interior which can cause the mantle molten and move, the movement of the upper core liquid, the pressure underneath the crust, Sun light, earth magnetic field, and all the activities carried by the biolife on it whose interactions and inter-effect are identified as of an ecosystem. The earth as a whole is a self-regulating ecosystem as well. In fact the whole universe is an unlimited-domain of ecosystem which expands both outwardly and inwardly upon observation.

The earth's ecosystems, the interactions among plants, animals, microorganisms and the soil, water, the atmosphere and sunlight on the earth is a cycle chain. If any block of the cycle is broken, the whole systems can be broken and it can alter the overall conditions on the planet.

For quite a long time the Yang force has over taken, and the balance has been over stretched since the industrial revolution and particularly in the last several dozens of years it is under severe challenge. The symptoms of the severe challenges are: short occurring frequency of large-scale earthquakes, severe weathers in disrupted patterns, the extinction trends of species, desertification, deforestation, climate change, glacier ice melting, sea level rise, air pollution etc. etc.

It is unfortunate but fair that any of the blocks on the cycle is both a factor to influence the whole cycle chain and also subject to its consequences. It is pinpointed that human activities are of the main responsibility for the result of Yang force taking over so far.

The land on the earth used to be covered by endless forestry, bushes, pastures which directly provided shelters and food supply for millions of species including human beings. Photosynthesis of the plants while producing oxygen for all lives on Earth also takes in carbon dioxide from the air produced from all the activities on earth as a purifier. Everything that was created originally by the nature's mighty hands is good and logical. It is observed and also proved by scientific experiments and study to which human's minds are bound to acceptance, that excessive industrial usage and cultivation of land, mining and drilling have resulted in massive areas of deforestation and desertification all over the globe which have driven millions of animals out of their natural habitat, further caused the atmospheric temperature rising, and may also add more heat beneath the earth surface that in return can change the earth interior pressure, glacier melting; the energy thirst from intense human activities has been compelling human beings madly drill on the earth everywhere they can access and the drillings go deeper and deeper. These drillings inevitably make the earth interior structures and pressure nearby deviate, which would lead to the distribution of the whole earth's mass and pressure losing balance. In order to release the unbalanced pressure, the earth has to find ways to ease itself. Therefore more frequent large scale earthquakes may be one of the direct consequences of the drillings. The waste gases from burning the fossil fuel by a large human population have increased the air temperature and pollution. More frequent cyclones, typhoons, storms, wildfires and other severe weathers you experience today may be cries of the earth to the temperature rise.

Today's occurring frequency of earthquakes becomes thousand times higher than in 18th century before or around the start of Industrial Revolution

Data shown in 18th century, apart from the 50s and 80s in which 5 and 4 earthquakes happened respectively, in every 10 years there were about 1-2 above Magnitude 5 earthquakes only; it totaled about 30 occurrences in the whole century.

While the first half of 19th century, every 10 years there were 3 or 4 earthquakes, and from 50s to end of the century, 5 - 7 in every 10 years. Earthquakes above magnitude 6 showed in records every year in 19th century; and the total occurrences almost doubled compared to that in 18th century.

20th century and the beginning of 21st century witnessed acceleration in earthquake happening frequency. Below are the data for 2000-2012 located by the US Geological Survey National Earthquake Information Center.

Chart 1#

Magnitude	2000	2001	2002	2003	2004	2005	2006	2007	2008	2009	2010	2011	2012
8.0 to 9.9	1	1	0	1	2	1	2	4	0	1	1	1	2
7.0 to 7.9	14	15	13	14	14	10	9	14	12	16	23	19	12
6.0 to 6.9	146	121	127	140	141	140	142	178	168	144	150	185	108
5.0 to 5.9	1344	1224	1201	1203	1515	1693	1712	2074	1768	1896	2209	2276	1401
4.0 to 4.9	8008	7991	8541	8462	10888	13917	12838	12078	12291	6805	10164	13315	9534
3.0 to 3.9	4827	6266	7068	7624	7932	9191	9990	9889	11735	2905	4341	2791	2453
2.0 to 2.9	3765	4164	6419	7727	6316	4636	4027	3597	3860	3014	4626	3643	3111
1.0 to 1.9	1026	944	1137	2506	1344	26	18	42	21	26	39	47	43
0.1 to 0.9	5	1	10	134	103	0	2	2	0	1	0	1	0
No Magnitude	3120	2807	2938	3608	2939	864	828	1807	1922	17	24	11	3
Total	22256	23534	27454	31419	31194	30478	29568	29685	31777	14825	21577	*22289	*16667

25

When compared with the information for 18th and 19th century, it tells not only there are hundreds, even thousands of times more large scale earthquakes in recent years, but also reveals on much more frequency of small scale (below Mag5) quakes. If the technology for quake detection is considered, there may be significant difference in small earthquake records. However earthquakes with magnitude above 5 were unlikely missed for records since it could be felt by all who were in the quake areas. Therefore there should not be much missing data in the 18th -19th century for them.

These figures are astonishing! From 1-2 in every 10 years to hundreds, even over 2 thousand occurrences each year just over two hundred and fifty years passed, how comes!

Below is the latest data according to Wikipedia which include data for 2013. You can see by no mistakes how big impact that human activities laid on earthquake happenings. The two highest figures in 2007 and 2011 closely relate to the two peaks in economic activity in human society.

Chart 2#

26

Number of Earthquakes Worldwide for 2000–2013

Magnitude Ranging Between	2000	2001	2002	2003	2004	2005	2006	2007	2008	2009	2010	2011	2012	2013
8–9.9	1	1	0	1	2	1	2	4	0	1	1	1	2	2
7–7.9	14	15	13	14	14	10	9	14	12	16	21	19	15	17
6–6.9	146	121	127	140	141	140	142	178	168	144	151	204	129	124
5–5.9	1344	1224	1201	1203	1515	1693	1712	2074	1768	1896	1963	2271	1412	1402
Total	1505	1361	1341	1358	1672	1844	1865	2270	1948	2057	2136	2495	1558	1545

Who can deny that it is human activity that has brought most of these catastrophic events on Earth which is the habitat for millions of species including human beings yourselves?!

The depth of oil well drilling gets deeper and deeper and fossil fuel consumption hits skyscrapers

According to EIA and US EIA, the world crude oil consumption rose to pass 90 million barrels per day and continues its rising trend. The CO_2 emission reached another record at 36 billion metric tons per year and will follow the oil consumption trend.

In 1949 the earliest year with data available, it shows the US annual average depth of oil wells drilled was 3,635 feet, now the average depth of well drilling is between 8000-9000 feet.

The U.S. consumes 18.89 million barrels of petroleum each day in 2013 -- almost half of it in the form of gasoline. The agency says, by 2035, U.S. total consumption per day is estimated to total 21.9 billion barrels. And the Carbon Dioxide emission in 1980 was 4.78 million metric tons, while in 2007 its economic peak it rose to 6.03 million metric tons, and since the recession it dropped to 5.5 million metric tons in 2011, but regained 2% in 2013.

China, back in 1980 which was the beginning of its economic growth, consumed 1.76 million barrels per day. With its economic growth it consumed 10.70 million barrels each day in 2013 and its Carbon dioxide emission from 1.45 million metric tons in 1980 rose to about 9.7 million metric tons in 2013.

These are just data from two countries. There are 21 other countries that each consumes 1-5 million barrels per day. You can imagine how much thirst has been driving the mad drilling and how much CO_2 emission in total has been released and continues increasing to release into the air that all lives on the Earth rely on to breathe. *Human beings, it's time to wake up!*

According to BP report released 15 Jan 2014, the global energy consumption is expected to rise by 41 per cent from 2012 to 2035, and mainly driven by emerging economies - led by China and India, followed by the Middle East. Shares of the major fossil fuels of oil, natural gas and coal still a major with each making up to around 27% of the total mix 81% by 2035, and the remaining share of global energy consumption coming from nuclear, hydroelectricity and renewable. And by 2035 the number of cars on road will be 1.7 billion, by then how much more oil consumption and CO_2 emission will be, do you even want to think of that? **Humans, How can you allow this model of life on earth continue to poison your own life?**

Another factor that may contribute to unbalanced distribution of the earth mass is the centralized industrial cities, and commercial, densely populated cities which

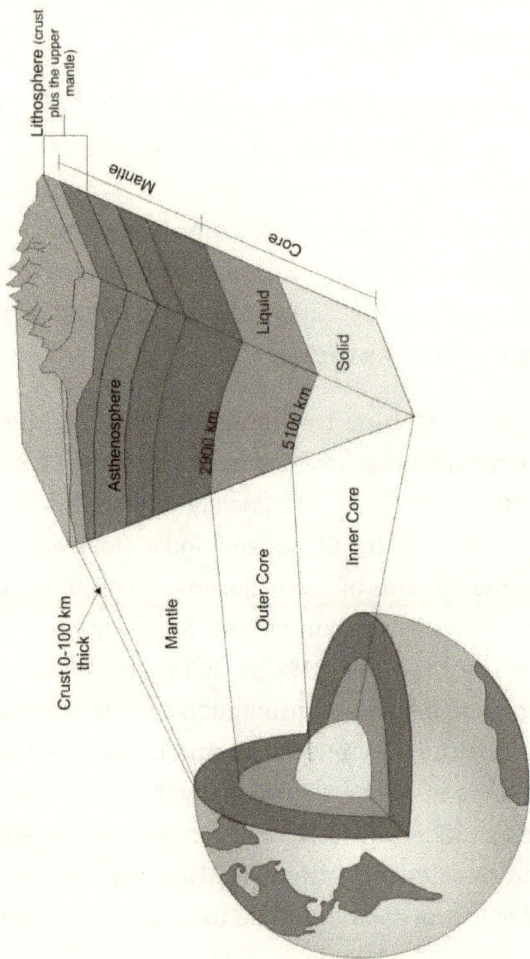

Fig 6#

30

host millions of human population, and which guarantees releasing waste gases in concentrated areas; and moreover the heavy high rises in each city have just gotten higher and higher. You can imagine, on a much smaller ground base one a few hundred to a few thousand feet tall building with steel and concrete is erected, loading all its thousands of tons of weight on one concentrated earth area. How can it not to disturb the normal distribution of the mass and interior pressure of the earth? The earth is like a well boiled egg – the shell is its crust, the white is its mantle and yolk is its core, except that the earth's crust probably is more elastic than the egg shell. In order to simulate the effect to show what happens, you can use a boiled egg without the shell peeled, put a pressure on the egg with your fingers, you will see it goes down where you place the pressure and push the egg mass to the sides. Similar effect with the earth, heavy tall buildings place a lot pressure on its surface, the building weight would push down the earth surface but you probably do not notice, and the pressure built up below the surface thus push aside the mass in upper mantle. The difference between a well-boiled egg and the earth is that there is always likely somewhere that is weak in the crust of the earth especially along the continental plates, then the energy built up from the pressure would seek to release through the weak points in the form of earthquakes, volcanoes, landslides etc. in order for the earth to balance itself.

Humans, why do you have to chase the name No 1? Your

buildings go higher and higher, but you do not know the surface under your feet goes lower and lower till one day it cannot endure anymore and release its anger through destructive behaviors! It is like a person who has been given a lot of hits, at the beginning he tries to take all in to bear it until one day the pain and the pressure built-up in his heart come to a point that he cannot endure anymore if he wants to live, so he releases his pain and anger by the explosion of violence in all kinds of ways. The Earth has been crying for help for such a long time, but it seems nobody living on it has heard of it, nobody would pay attention to it or nobody could do anything to change it even though some may have noticed it!

Explosion of human population adds another heavy fist to the pain and push the already off-track engine on a mal-circle.

According to United Nation's statistics, in year 1800 there were around 1 billion human population on Earth, 1900 around 1.7 billion. In 1950 it reached 2.5 billion, from then on human population shoots like a rocket. As of March 26, 2014, it is estimated to number 7.168 billion by the United States Census Bureau (USCB). According to UN, birth number is now expected to remain at their 2011 level of 134 million, while death number 56 million per year. The global population is expected to become between 8.3 and 10.9 billion by 2050. But there is also a risk for a much bigger number if it is not steadily brought under control.

China, India are the two countries that have a population exceeding 1 billion each, followed by United states, Indonesia, Brazil, Pakistan, Bangladesh, Nigeria, Russia and Japan that exceed 100 million each. If the growth trend of the population is not halted, what the overall situations on Earth will be, you can imagine!

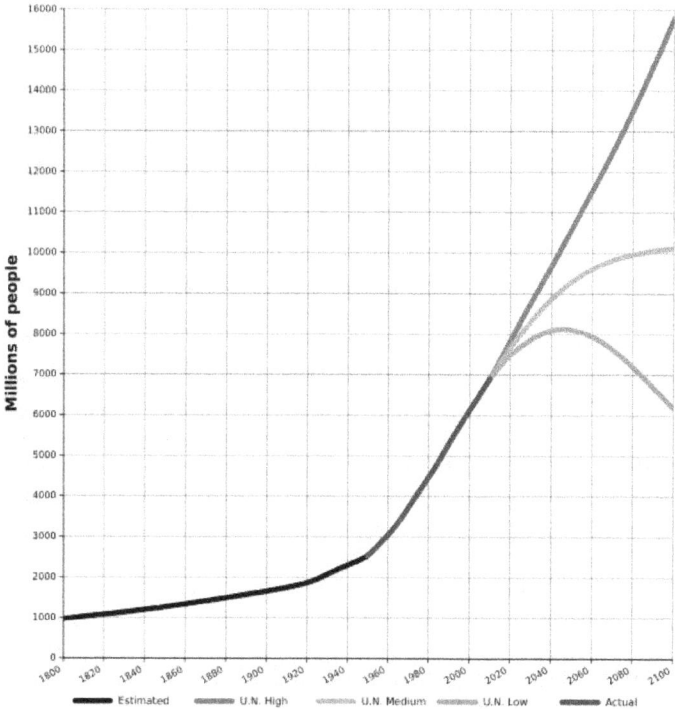

Fig.7

Human beings as a species is one of the blocks in the ecosystem on Earth. The earth to maintain a healthy and sustainable self-regulated system for all lives on it which includes plants, all other animals and human beings, marian lives, and healthy air, soil, water plus adequate sunlight, it requires each of the blocks in the system fit into its proposition of the whole system by both supplying and taking energy resources in the cycle. Any of the blocks too weak or too strong would break its overall conditions.

It is identified that the exploded human population directly results in over exploitation of resources from other blocks on the ecosystem. To be specific, as a result of over population, vast land of natural forestries and green pastures were deprived of millions of other species, and converted into farms, human dwellings and factories, which have been driving wild animals to extinction or near to extinction, or being directly over-consumed by humans, in return it has killed the abundance of food supply to all lives. The loss of forests, pastures and bush forests leaves the earth insufficient resources to support an adequate photosysnthsis with which plants, algae and organisms breathe in carbon dioxide and release oxygen into the air which are required for all lives on Earth to survive. The explosive human population has a 2-way deficiency in this ecosystem in the forms of decreasing the sources for regenerating supplies and increasing unobsorbable human waste to the environment. The overly supplied carbon dioxide from fossil fuel burning and transportation emissions increases the green house effect which in turn causes the air temperature rising and depletion of ozone layer; the air gets thinner and thinner, then leading to more sunlight and ultravoilet enter into the atmosphere which can cause direct damage to life forms exposed to it, and again causing the air temperature rise; air temperature rise in return causes more water vaporation into the air which leads to more turbulant weather conditions like curricans, typhones, storm, floods etc.

Everybody knows how different the air is if you stay in a wood compared to standing on an open area without any tree in a very hot day in summer. The temperature rise in the air plus strong sunlight on large bulk land then causes soil erosion that may damage the conditions for crop growth for food supply. Again a lot of animals are dying off from the environmental change of their natural habitats. This malcycle can go on and on forever. It is like that you are digging a tomb for yourself.

It is believed that the air temperature could exceed historical analogs as early as 2047 affecting most ecosystems on the earth and marine systems if no immediate actions are taken, therefore without exception all lives on the earth will take severe consequences.

The world's last Passenger Pigeon, once belonging to one of the most abundant species, died on September 1, 1914, at the Cincinnati Zoon. The birds lived in enormous migratory flocks until the early 20th century when hunting and habitat destruction led to its demise. People once described in 1866 a flock of them in southern Ontario, being as 1 mi (1.5 km) wide and 300 mi (500 km) long, took 14 hours to pass, and numbered in excess of 3.5 billion birds.

The population of Yangtzi dolphin, also called Whitefin, a fresh water dolphin seen only in the Yangtze River in China, declined drastically in decades as China industrialized and made heavy use of the river for fishing, transportation, and hydroelectricity. Conservation efforts were made to save the species, but in late 2006 they were failed in being spotted in the river and declared functionally extinct.

Human population explosion and ruthless depriving the life of other species are a result of a belief system that plays in human's mind

This undesirable result is deeply rooted in the fact that human beings as a species hold a belief that they are the ruler of the world, the 'dominion force' over all other species instead of being one of the blocks in a complete life circle on Earth due to ignorance about the nature and themselves, and misleading from religious sources. More specifically they regard animals inferior on a linear chain of life (while they sit on the top) created by God for them to control and 'enjoy' in any way with their will, and they regard plants as lower ranks and a supplementary pleasure to their eyes and at their free disposal with their will. They regard the earth, and other celestial bodies as non-living objects in the sky instead of different forms of life and still searching for lives identical to themselves in the space.

In Buddhism there are six hierarchical realms that human beings would take for rebirth according to their karma accumulated while they are alive on earth, and animal realm is no3# below realm of human beings just above Preta which is dwelled by hungry ghosts. These concepts have been rooted in the mind of a lot of people in Asia where Buddhist culture are a main influence in society. There can be a lot of proofs easily picked up in every aspects of their culture such as languages. Here is a saying in Chinese: "you are not even as good as a pig nor a dog" which they would use when they curse someone they think are 'bad' or may have done something bad to them. Another: "you bastard with a wolf-heart and a dog-lung!" which is so explicit therefore no need to elaborate!

In traditional Christian teachings, it was believed that God created animals and other living beings for humans to use as food supply and bring total control with their will. This teaching seems having scripture backups:

In Genesis 1.26 " Then God said, 'Let us make humankind in our image, according to our likeness; and let them have dominion over the fish of the sea, and over the birds of the air, and over the cattle, and over all the wild animals of the earth, and over every creeping thing that creeps upon the earth."

1.28 God blessed them (to humankind), and God said to them, 'Be fruitful and multiply, and fill the earth and subdue it; and have dominion over the fish of the sea and over the birds of the air and over every living thing that moves upon the earth.'

Did God really want Humankind be one superior dominion over other beings? Absolutely not! It is human's own mind making the interpretation of the scriptures. When you read chapter 1.29 and 1.30, you would immediate rethink and take more ponder on the above scriptures:

1.29 "God said, 'See, I have given you every plant yielding seed that is upon the face of all the earth, and every tree with seed in its fruit; you shall have them for food. 1.30 And to every beast of the earth, and to every bird of the air, and to everything that creeps on the earth, everything that has the breath of life, I have given every green plant for food.' And it was so"

1.29 and 1.30, God said every plant produce from the earth should be used as food for human beings as well as for all other living beings on the earth. He did not say only human beings should have them for food, instead saying 'and to every beast, and to every bird, and to every fish, and to everything that has life'. Animals have equal rights to enjoy the produce from the earth.

The words 'subdue' 'dominion' have slight variations in

meaning, here in the scripture they should be understood as 'to bring under cultivation' and 'exercise management'

From verse 1.28, you will see what has gone wrong with the scripture and the development of human beings:

The New Revised Standard Version (Anglicized Edition)

28God blessed them, and God said to them, 'Be fruitful and multiply, and fill the earth and subdue it; and have dominion over the fish of the sea and over the birds of the air and over every living thing that moves upon the earth.'

New International Version
God blessed them and said to them, "Be fruitful and increase in number; fill the earth and subdue it. Rule over the fish in the sea and the birds in the sky and over every living creature that moves on the ground."

New Living Translation
Then God blessed them and said, "Be fruitful and multiply. Fill the earth and govern it. Reign over the fish in the sea, the birds in the sky, and all the animals that scurry along the ground."

English Standard Version
And God blessed them. And God said to them, "Be fruitful and multiply and fill the earth and subdue it, and have dominion over the fish of the sea and over the birds of the heavens and over every living thing that

moves on the earth."

New American Standard Bible
God blessed them; and God said to them, "Be fruitful and multiply, and fill the earth, and subdue it; and rule over the fish of the sea and over the birds of the sky and over every living thing that moves on the earth."

Now read carefully the **King James Version** *(1604-1611),* which is one of the earliest English translation available and see the big difference with all the latest versions:

28 And God blessed them, and God said unto them, Be fruitful, and multiply, and **replenish** the earth, and subdue it: and have dominion over the fish of the sea, and over the fowl of the air, and over every living thing that moveth upon the earth.

'replenish' and 'fill', what a big difference between these two words! God wants you to take care of the Earth by nurturing it, replenishing it to make it renewable instead of simply exploiting it by filling it with your own offspring only.

With the time passing and the lost of old texts, the very important message was lost in the pass-ons and translations for various reasons

It is very clear that God wants humans to exercise management, on behalf of Him, as a manager, not letting the whole system run out or over flow, or run bad, and giving all beings equal rights to share various supply and abundance on the earth. You all hate it when a CEO of a large corporation immensely profits his own pocket by taking advantage of his prescribed management position which may result in bankruptcy of the company, sooner or later the CEO would have to be removed by the board. Similarly, as one of the blocks of species on a life circle and a pointed manager of this circle, human's population should not have any privileges and exceptions over other species, nor as traditionally understood 'to multiply infinitely' at any circumstances, as a result eating up all the resources for the whole earth family.

It is all about the individual consciousness in understanding the messages and the nature. However it is a tendency for human's mind to exercise control over others (will be elaborated in next tier massage) which conduces to the misleading in traditional teaching and to the demise of other lives on Earth.

Even in the scriptures of Bhagavad Gita, which I believe containing the most enlightened messages about human beings and the universe, animals are regarded in lower abode, being left in a vulnerable position. In chapter 14.14 and 14.15 when elaborating the three modes of material nature and the outcomes, it goes like:

"When one dies in the mode of goodness, he attains to the pure higher planets of the great sages".

"When one dies in the mode of passion, he takes birth among those engaged in fruition activities; and when one dies in the mode of ignorance, he takes birth in the animal kingdom"

However there were individual saints in Christian history who were sensitive to and treated animals as equal, like Saint Francis Assisi who talked with a wolf and made peace between the wolf and people of Gubbio.

A great soul of the late 19th-20th century had the intention to change the situation. One day when he was visiting Kali temple in West Bengal, Mahatma Gandhi encountered and wrote in Chapter 72 of his Auto Biography:

"On the way I saw a stream of sheep going to be sacrificed to kali temple. And I spoke to a worshiper.

"I asked him: 'Do you regard this sacrifice as religion?'

'Who would regard killing of animals as religion?'

'Then, why don't you preach against it?'

'That's not my business. Our business is to worship God.'

'But could you not find any other place in which to worship God?'

'All places are equally good for us. The people are like a flock of sheep, following where leaders lead them. It is no business of us #sadhus#.'

We did not prolong the discussion but passed on to the temple. We were greeted by rivers of blood. I could not bear to stand there. I was exasperated and restless. I have never forgotten that sight. That very evening I had an invitation to dinner at a party of Bengali friends. There I spoke to a friend about this cruel form of worship. He said: 'The sheep don't feel anything. The noise and the drum-beating there deaden all sensation of pain.'

I could not swallow this. I told him that, if the sheep had speech, they would tell a different tale. I felt that the cruel custom ought to be stopped. I thought of the story of Buddha, but I also saw that the task was beyond my capacity. I hold today the opinion as I held then. To my mind the life of a lamb is no less precious than that of a human being. I should be unwilling to take the life of a lamb for the sake of the human body. I hold that, the more helpless a creature, the more entitled it is to protection by man from the cruelty of man. But he who has not qualified himself for such service is unable to afford to it any protection. I must go through more self-purification and sacrifice before I can hope to save these lambs from this unholy sacrifice. Today I think I must die pining for this self-purification and sacrifice. It is my constant prayer that there may be born on earth some great spirit, man or woman, fired with divine pity, who will deliver us from this heinous sin, save the lives of the innocent creatures, and purify the temple. How is it that Bengal with all its knowledge, intelligence, sacrifice, and emotion tolerates this slaughter?"

But unfortunately the mainstream of traditional Christian teachings regarded animals as inferior that resulted in distorted belief in the mind of majority of people. And a lot of people believe that animals, plants do not have feelings and thoughts, and they see a lot of life forms as non-living things. But even the 'non-living' things have feelings and thoughts.

How can you not see from their eyes, from their reactions and all various sounds they make that there are intelligence and feelings in them and they always try to communicate with human beings? Just because they do not use the same languages as you do? How many great stories about animals that have moved so many people, no matter domestic or wild? It is so easy to name them, be it the three famous lions in different times: the lioness Elsa and her cubs, the lion Christine, and the most sophisticated lioness Maditau on Duba Island. Many may have heard that after a conservationist and author Lawrence Anthony passed away, although without being alerted to the event, a group of wild elephants Anthony helped to rescue and rehabilitate travelled for miles to his house in South Africa for a 2-day vigil or mourning.

Animals do speak, but in their own languages. If you pay attention to the nature, watch all around you, you will see a much lively world and notice more, feel more. Above all there is a universal language with which inter species can communicate – that is the Spirit which is ALL That Is, which dwells in all beings, moving and nonmoving.

There is a well-made documentary on animal (interspecies) communication featured Anne Breytenbach who works as a bridge between humans and other species. Through connection in energy field, Anne receives images and body sensations from those animals she communicates with and translates them into verbal languages back to people concerned. The human species has the ability as well to communicate with other beings at the origin of the creation, but on the course of its development, this innate ability sadly was left behind locked in a corner. You need to reclaim that innate ability if you want to take your assigned duty as a proper manager in the whole global ecosystem. But the first step you need to change is your belief system, and see all lives as equal on earth, and broaden your view of life forms in the whole cosmos.

Take heed from dinosaur extinction, adjust human's over heated activities, return the Yin Yang balance to the earth

Dinosaurs lived on the earth from 231.4 million to 66 million years ago. Then it was over a geologically short period of time 66 million years ago during a mass extinction event, all non-avian dinosaurs plus some three-quarters of plant and animal species on Earth were wiped out.

When Dinosaur first appeared on the earth, the land was in a single supercontinent, it was only around 180 million years ago it began to break apart. Dinosaurs were various dominant groups of over 1000 non-avian species animals living on earth for about 165 million years spreading on the single continent. A lot of them were gigantic, the largest dinosaur might have been 58 meters (190 feet) long, and 9.25 meters (30 feet 4 inches) tall. It is believed during that time, the atmospheric temperatures were much hotter than today, there were no pole ice caps, the temperatures at north pole were about 50 °C (90 °F) warmer than today. That's why it nourished so many gigantic living creatures. The sea level was also 100-250 feet higher than today.

Why were the atmospheric temperatures much higher than today? Why were there no pole ice caps? Was it because the earth was slightly closer to the sun or its axis was different from today? It is believed that the earth temperature was quite uniform, about 25 °C(45°F). Wasn't it not possible that the dominant dinosaurs gradually destroyed the earth ecosystem and had changed the climate so that it disturbed the Earth energy field therefore altered either its orbit or axis dramatically, as a consequence it caused a catastrophic event and brought the demise to 98% its number and 2/3 of all other species?

There was another mass extinction event at about 300 million years ago which Scientists believe it might have been attributed to plant dominance.

It looked like whenever there was one single species or group prevalent on Earth there would have linked to an extinction event, which might happen in a geographic period of time or a very rapid process like the last one with non-avian dinosaur's extinction. In the history of life evolution on Earth there were 4-5 major extinction events which had happened in intervals between about 100-150 million years. However by now it has been only 66 million years since the last event of vast extinction on Earth.

In my childhood in the nineteen seventies, a lot of birds were seen in the sky in Beijing, but now you barely spot a single one of them in the neighborhoods.

At present there are hundreds of species either endangered or threatened to extinction, such as Asian tigers, lions, elephants, rhinos, leopards, African wild dogs, gorilla, whales, bluefin tuna, giant panda etc.

Human beings always believe they are the most intelligent beings on Earth. It may be true that with the expansion of consciousness of human species, more and more of you have already sensed the urgency of the situation, or if you are starting to realize that in order to survive on this beautifully and intricately created planet by the Divine force, and which has been given to all created beings on Earth and required all beings to function properly within this ecosystem. It is not difficult to get there, you just need to learn to respect other beings and the whole earth environment, and make yourself fit into this system meanwhile being a watch dog for the earth and a proper manager for God, making sure its Yin Yang balance won't be over stretched or not for a prolonged time, lest the Nature, Law of Balance, the Divine would take its course by force.

"天地不仁，以万物为刍狗 Heaven and Earth do not show mercy (by taking preference), they see all things as pure and holy." - Laozi, TaoTeJing

Chapter 3

Message Tier No.3

The Truth is revealed: over-heated Yang force in an individual human being blinds him to see the whole picture, causing him sufferings; as a result, unbalanced Yin Yang forces in human society lead humankind astray

The two-in-One, One in two Taiji symbol can be applied in describing any domains in the universe representing the two polarized forces in conformity under One Unified Force, from Macro cosmos, through human society, human's body, to micro molecules, atoms, and subatomic particles. With the change of the domains, the Yin Yang forces represented as different elements or forms would evolve to the opposite direction, and even in the same form the Yin Yang elements constantly evolve according to conditions. This is the essence of the Yin-Yang Changes (see Book of Changes), and this essential characteristic correlates to Einstein's relativity theory

The Yin force is characterized with elements that are Manifested, Crystallized, Still, Calm, Cool, Peaceful, Orderly, Soft, Negative, Heavy, Passive, Dark, Female,

Woman, etc.

The Yang force is characterized with elements that are Unmanifested, Vibrational, Energetic, Dynamic, Hot, Restless, Chaotic, Hard, Positive, Light, Active, White, Male, Man etc.

The concept of Yin-Yang energy in a human's body and the importance of Yin energy in life creation

When God created humankind, He created them with both Yin and Yang energies in them which denotes the meaning of harmonious union of them in God, and he placed emphasis on Yin energy in Creation and in the role of bringing in harmony. These notions were depicted in different creation myths and cultures around the world:

In Chinese Legends, Fuxi (male) and NuWa (female) were primordial human beings, they were sometimes depicted in images of human bodies with dragon/serpent tails in one picture (yin-yang union). Legend says after Pangu created Heaven and Earth, plants, birds and animals, Nuwa, a female creature with human head and serpent body was walking on the land. She felt lonely, so by the river according to her own image she made humans with clay. And later Nuwa refined five-color pebbles to mend the hole in heaven resulted from the fight between god of water and god of fire with flood rushing onto the earth from heaven, symbolizing the restoration of life.

Fig8#

Fig9#

In Greek mythology, Gaia, the personification of the Earth, the primal Mother Goddess, also gave birth to the Earth and the Universe. Gaia brought forth Uranus (heaven, sky), and from union with Uranus, she gave birth to all heavenly gods and deities, and the giants.

The Chinese cardinal philosophy of Yin Yang forces in a human body is originated and orally passed down from Emperor Huangdi about 5000 years ago and recorded as a full series of medical books – The Classic of Human Body/ Huangdi Inner Books about 400-200BCE. The philosophy believes Qi is the spirit in a human body, it is received from the heaven and earth in the forms of Yin and Yang energies that nourish different organs and meridians of the body. If Yin and Yang lose balances, diseases would arise in a human body. Another example, the Chinese word '人' (person) is written in two strokes in a manner that denotes the meaning of male and female supporting each other and together making a complete person.

In chapter 6, DaoTeJing, it says:

谷神不死，是谓玄牝；玄牝之门，是谓天地根；绵绵若存，用之不绝。

The female spirit never dies, it is the Mother of mysteries;

The door to Mother of mysteries is to the root (knowledge) of heaven and earth;

It exists in abundance, never exhausts

In Hindu culture, kundalini Shakti is the female energy that is believed coiled at the base of a human's spine, when it is activated it would generate powerful life forces and go up along the spine to reunite with Shiva, the male energy at the crown to achieve spiritual truth. Along the spine of a human body, there are seven energy centers, the chakras which are the connection points for inner and outer energy to flow through and nurture the inner organs and meridians of the body.

In Geneses 1.27, it also indicates that the Yin Yang

energies were injected to human beings:

So God created humankind in his image,

in the image of God He created them;

male and female He created them.

From the name of the Man and Woman first created by God in Genesis, it unmistakably conveys the conception of Yin-Yang energy:

Adam, 'אדם' in Hebrew associated with 'Red', the color representing passion, desire, and love as well as energy, war, danger, strength, power. It resembles the characteristics of Yang energy

Eve, ה י ח (haya) in Hebrew meaning 'to live, to have life, to give or restore life'. It represents the Yin energy, God-like energy

More interestingly, if you look inside your own body, DNA, a molecule that encodes the genetic instructions used in the development and functioning of all known living organisms and many viruses, contains two strands running opposite directions to each other. The DNA-helix was discovered only recently compared to the long history of all life including first humo sapiens appeared on Earth. It is very likely that scientists will discover some more valuable information within DNA which may indicate the differences between the subtle Yin -Yang energies in an individual body because this is a universal law.

You are Eternal Beings, manifested in your crystallized flesh body, will be reborn into another flesh or permanently dwell in the Spiritual Realm after this life time

Before the Truth is unveiled before your eyes, you need to know who you are, why you come to this world.

Everything you know in this world by the normal senses is energy at its core but in different forms, and everything is dynamic, constantly evolves through vibrations at microscopic domains and constantly transforms its forms. Take your body for example, even while you are asleep, your heart is still beating (this is not microscopic), the cells of your body are still in a state of transforming into blood the energy that you have taken in as food, water, sunlight etc. and the blood is nurturing your body silently, and the next day when you get up with the freshened energy, you may have a new life vision, or to finish a project at hand. Moreover, and usually ignored, while your body is not moving, but the earth is moving by orbiting and rotating, and the sun is orbiting the center of the milky way galaxy, the galaxy is orbiting, and so on, so in all these multilayered movements, your body's energy is in constant interaction with that of the whole universe. The interaction of this subtle energy plays a substantial role in an individual life, human society, animal society and the whole universe, which is observed and found explanation in Metaphysics and Quantum Physics. Another e.g. with a pile of wood, some nails, a hammer plus your thought you can choose to make a table, a ladder or something else you need. Energy and forms convert to each other.

The whole universe is in two complete overlapping Realms as a Unified Whole, Oneness Existence – the visible physical realm and the invisible Spiritual Realm. The manifest and the unmanifest: mass and energy convert to each other, and this is an eternal evolving pattern of life generation. The matter generated in the present cycle may be different in forms from a previous one, and this is a life cycle in both micro and macro scope of the universe. Without either of the two worlds, the universe won't exist. The Whole, Oneness Existence is God Consciousness which permeates everywhere and in everything in the entire universe, and holds the two realms together. It is so intricate, so abundant, but so orderly organized that no one knows where it starts and where it ends, and no one name can describe its opulence. Because it is so common, exists in all creations, it can be recognized by its core principle, again symbolized by the Taiji Ball.

The visible physical realm, the world, usually perceived by the normal five senses, emotions and mind, is resembled by the manifestations of all forms in shape, living and nonliving matters, such as stars, planets, animals, humans, plants, insects, mountains, rivers etc. which can be seen, touched, smelled, heard and tasted, and constitute relatively lower frequency of vibration in the form of energy. In this world the perception of human's mind is governed by the principle of duality in which the mind sees everything in a linear state, as black versus white, evil versus good, ugly versus beautiful, low versus high etc.

The invisible spiritual realm which can be sensed or perceived by the soul, the third eye through the energy field is exemplified by light and the sense of universal love, the sense of connection with all other existence in the universe, which had been demonstrated by Great Spiritual Masters in history like Krishna, Buddha, Jesus Christ, and a state described by a lot of ordinary people through Near Death Experiences, which constitute higher frequency of vibration. The elements in this realm are shapeless, formless, no time and space limit, moving at light or ultra-light speed, are pure energy. In this world mind becomes capitalized Universal Mind with which the perception is in unlimited dimensions, and it is governed by the principle of unity, wholeness, non-duality within which nothing is absolute which means everything is constantly evolving. There is no right or wrong, white or black, good or evil etc., therefore judgment has no sense; and there is no separation, everything connects to everything else, everything is interwoven together, and everything becomes pure existence. This is the Unnamable, Wuji, No Limit, state of Infinity. You can call it God, Supreme Spirit or whatever you want to call. But the moment you name it you limit it and limit yourself from Creation.

The principle of these characteristics in the spiritual realm correlates to and was crystallized as the theory of relativity (general and special) in physics by the great conscious mind, Albert Einstein. The principal theory states that measurements of various quantities are relative to the velocities of observers with space and time changed. This has profound meaning and it has shifted the old beliefs in human's everyday life. At a quantum level each person, as a life participant and observer, stays at a different space time, therefore the results of each person's observation is different, because thoughts are energy which interacts with other energies in the universe through vibration, especially those in the surrounding environment. And this would explain why different people have different views about the same things at the same time and place; and why the same person would change his mind on things with time changing. Therefore you should be aware that everything you hold in your belief system is relative, neither permanent nor absolute.

Think about - if those pioneered individual conscious minds in history had not been open enough to challenge existing beliefs, today you might still think that the Sun is orbiting the earth.

The Supreme Truth exists outside and inside of all living beings, the moving and the nonmoving. Because He is subtle, He is beyond the power of the material senses to see or to know. Although far, far away, He is also near to all."

- Bhagavad Gita 13.16

So each human being, as well as all other living beings, by the Supreme Conscious Mind, is seeded from the same elements in cosmic dusts with a fraction of the Eternal Spirit or Super Soul, after choosing parents according to the assigned task or you may call it mission, imbedded in the mother's womb as an embryo, when the embryo grows mature, the individual Spirit (or Soul) takes birth to the physical world as a child; after the child is born into this material world, he starts to be gradually subject to the conditions of the human society in this physical world with a dual view, and when his journey in this physical world ends he will return to the spiritual world.

During this physical life time, the individual Spirit needs to find out what his assigned task, i.e. his purpose is and find the way to manifest it. If he cannot find out his life purpose and his behaviors are not aligned up with his Spirit, it will cause him pain, sufferings, troubles till his body is dissolved (die) from this physical world without his life purpose fulfilled; after his body dies he will take rebirth in next life cycle and continue to the fulfillment of his life purpose; while some people have fulfilled their life purpose, i.e. the reunion of his body and Spirit or nearly fulfilled. After his body is dissolved from this physical world, he may not take rebirth on his will, like some great masters and sages in history unless he chooses to reincarnate to this physical world with a new body to help other souls to find their purposes.

What does that mean when we say 'humankind was created in God's image'? Please do not take it literally as God has a physical image. No, God has no image physically, this 'image' refers to God's Consciousness – the characteristics of this non-dual consciousness constitute the qualities of no judgment, equality, freedom, infinity, and unconditional love in human's perspective, ever evolving, and these qualities are deeply encrypted in each individual's heart as Divine Laws when he is created. Should these laws be infringed they will have to be set right, retribution has to be paid. Since these laws are written in human's hearts and they are pulling you from the heart, you always crave for these qualities, and obviously these laws have been broken in the entire human history from ancient times to today. Now it should not be very difficult to understand why there have been so many conflicts and wars in human history.

"All created beings have their source in these two natures. Of all that is material and all that is spiritual in this world, know for certain that I am both the origin and the dissolution"

-    *Bhagavad Gita,7.6*

Yang energy over took the Yin energy for too long in the whole recorded human history for thousands of years which has created a limited belief system in human's mind

In this physical world, individual human body and human society are two different domains in terms of Yin-Yang energy in play, however they are closely related to each other. Human bodies are the main basic cells in human society, other living beings including the environment on earth, objects in the space have some influence in human society, but human bodies are the main players. Therefore how healthy the society is, it mainly relies on the collective consciousness of human beings, which is a constant evolving result of the interplay of the Yin-Yang energies in thousands of millions of individual human bodies.

In the domain of human body, the Yang energy is the force that brings forth new individual life experiences, and always thrives for moving forward propelled by the urge of evolution; while the Yin energy always fights to hold back and keeps still and stable pulled by the gravity. If these two forces interact relatively in balance, the person would achieve harmony in his life procession, and either of the two forces if takes over the other for a prolonged time, there would be issues in an individual's life, and when those individuals in societies are in positions of authority and big influence, and the issues are not recognized, sooner or later, they will manifest as individual problems, crimes, social issues, even wars in the circumstance of human societies to extremity, no matter they are civil wars or cross border wars.

The symptoms of Yang force in a human body are ambitions, desires for power, dominion, control, glory, fame, success, wealth, expansion, preference etc. These ambitions and desires usually push the human body to dynamic activities and actions. When the desires and ambitions are well balanced with the Yin energy, they are a force to break through the statics that needs change and bring about new initiatives in life. It is usually labeled as 'Positive'. However if the desires and ambitions go beyond a certain point, they become lust, if possessed by which the individual would get bewildered in mind, blinded in heart thus it would lead him to destructive actions. In the case of influential individuals with authority and power it would bring social violence and wars in extremity.

The symptoms of Yin force in a human body are longings, hopes for peace, equality, justice, fairness, harmony and freedom etc. These longings and hopes usually enable the human body to resort to the state of calmness, stillness, endurance, however to a certain point, then it can transform to two totally opposite directions: It may take the direction towards passiveness, procrastination, hopelessness; on the other hand if the longings and hopes cannot be fulfilled in a certain period of time, the human body can transform to being dominated by Yang force energy, therefore taking actions characterized with Yang force to the extremity of destruction actions, such as violence, wars.

Guided by these principles, you can easily pick up any wars in human history no matter it was a civil war, or a cross border war, you call it a conquest war or an anti-invasion war, a revolution or a rebellion war. Typical examples of ambition driven wars were those medieval wars such as warring-state wars and Qin unification wars in China around 500 BCE– 221BCE; Roman Empire building and expansion wars around 500BCE-100AD in Europe, and the wars during recent Expansion of European Colonialism over the globe in 15th-20th century represented mainly by Portugal, Spain, Netherlands, Britain, France and Italy, to Asia, Africa, and North and South America, and the Russian empire expansion in 18th- early 20th century.

Wars resulted from Yin force transformation such as American Independence war, Latin American country Independence war, Asian, African wars of Independence throughout 18th,19th and 20th century. The Yin force transformation phenomenon could also be well presented by Rebellion wars between the changing hands of dynasties in the history of China.

But these are just documented wars, and what about those wars started well early, and described in ancient scriptures and myths passed down by narrations, if they were true?

Overplayed Yang Force Energy Can Be Traced Back to Bible, the Old Testament Which Formed an Elusive Belief System in the Mind of Humanity

Then I opened Genesis and Exodus again. To my astonishment, these two books, to me, are actually full accounts on how step by step Son of God became sons of man, and how sons of man have been slipping away from the Heavenly Garden and going astray from the pastures the True Oneness God prepared for all beings, led by the over-played Yang force energy in individual human bodies. These accounts were full of undesired deeds and roots to today's social mechanisms and problems created by sons of men, including crimes of murders, lies, plotting, invasions, adultery, deprivation, separation and segregation, etc. etc.!

There is one important point you need to understand and make known to yourself – how do you think ancient scriptures and myths came alive? In my opinion, they first arose from individual conscious minds who were those that might have had very close relationship with the Universal Conscious Mind, the true Oneness God. In respect to ancient scriptures, through minds of those individual wise men and prophets, images or messages were claimed coming from God revelations, then through them stories were passed down through generations to generations orally, and with time passing more contents might be added in or some got lost, and misplaced till one day written records were available to have them kept. However one Truth is that any flesh in this dual-mind controlled human society is subject to the physical world conditions, no one body could and can claim that he has completely reunite his flesh with his Spirit till the day the flesh is dissolved from this physical world. Any spiritual practitioners would know that you cannot be absolutely sure that every messages coming to you are from God, because there are a lot of energies at work all around you. So many times those messages are disguised with God's voice but actually from your own mind or influenced by other undesired energies. In terms of mythologies, stories might be inspired from the One Conscious Mind, but obviously carried elements of regional culture backgrounds, they reflect the life, thoughts of human beings in particular regions and spacetime, on their understanding about the creation, the relationship with gods, their custom, social activities etc.

In my opinion, many occasions in the events described in Genesis and Exodus were led by the Yang force energy but disguised with God's voice. The earliest Hebrew Bible scriptures were believed written by various men and only finalized around 3rd century BCE, and partly selected as Old Testament in Bible, and the New Testament scriptures were believed in completion by various men in the 1st century about 50-60 years after Jesus Christ died.

Humankind slipped into duality state led by Yang force, Human beings had been living in the heavenly Garden with abundance of fruit and food supply, also surrounded by other animals to share the food, and they did not know 'good or evil', which means their minds were of non-dual state, like God. Since God input Yin - Yang energy in them, and the Yang energy was always propelling because it wanted to know more and it wanted to be like 'God', so the serpent came to induce and asked "Did God say, 'You shall not eat from any tree in the garden'?", the woman said "We may eat of the fruit of the trees in the garden; but God said, 'You shall not eat of the fruit of the tree that is in the middle of the garden, nor shall you touch it, or you shall die'." . Then the serpent said to the woman, 'You will not die; for God knows that when you eat of it your eyes will be opened, and you will be like God, knowing good and evil.' *('God' here should be quotation marked or lower case, because duality is the state of demigods and men, the mind of Supreme God is non-dual)*

The serpent here in the scripture should be representing the Yang force energy instead of the commonly perceived 'evil' entity. In a lot of mythologies, serpents appeared and represented either power or wisdom in relation with gods and rulers. In Egypt, uraeus (serpent) as a golden emblem symbolizing power was worn on Pharaoh's head. In Chinese mythology, Fuxin and Nuwa the primordial of humankind were depicted with human head with serpent and dragon bodies (in fig.7).

In other mythologies, such as Scandinavia, Germany, Greece, South East Asian Countries, serpents and dragons were sometimes also used interchangeably.

Sons of God became sons of men led by Yang force, Adam and Eve, progenitors of humankind, came into being from God. God created Eve from Adam's rib implying the union of Yin-Yang forces in a human body. Abel, and Cain, and Seth came into being by God's Spirit:

Chapter 4.1-2   *Now the man knew his wife Eve, and she conceived and bore Cain, saying, 'I have produced a man with the help of the Lord.' 2 Next she bore his brother Abel…*

and all the sons and daughters in early generations came from God's Spirit till those days the Nephilim were on Earth when Sons of God went into the Daughters, and they became sons of men:

Chapter 6.1-4, Genesis, *"When people began to multiply on the face of the ground, and daughters were born to them, [2]the sons of God saw that they were fair; and they took wives for themselves of all that they chose. [3]Then the Lord said, 'My spirit shall not abide in mortals for ever, for they are flesh; their days shall be one hundred and twenty years.' ⁴The Nephilim were on the earth in those days - and also afterwards - when the sons of God went in to the daughters of humans, who bore children to them. These were the heroes that were of old, warriors of renown"*

When sons of God let their minds taken over by a single Yang force without the more god-like yin energy to balance it, lusts arose, when lust for flesh pleasure arose, more flesh without God's Spirit were produced. When Yang force took over, those 'giants' and 'heroes' in human's eyes were born on earth. Without God's Spirit, human's body is dead, therefore when Jesus came upon the earth he looked around the world and He saw a corpse, *'whoever see the world a corpse will not experience death'.*

Individual Consciousness to God Consciousness

How an individual balances the Yin and Yang forces depends on the relationship between his individual consciousness and God Consciousness. All beings come from the seed of God, are of Spirit beings, belonging to Spiritual Realm. However after an individual comes into being on the earth, since the Spirit - Self is of non-duality and the human mind in physical world is of duality, he is bombarded with all kinds of conceptions with respect to customaries, rituals, culture, religion etc in the society during the process of growing up; He does not feel ease with all these surround him, but he has to conform with the world in order to be 'accepted' in it by behaving 'normal', thus majority of them would form gradually a thick 'shield' – self and believe self is what He is, mixed up with the capitalized Self, the Spirit. Unfortunately each time a new 'learning' is obtained it also pushes the Spirit one step backward, and puts up a wall and a lock around him till he is pushed into a corner in the heart with layer after layer of walls and locks. Perhaps the rebellion behaviors in adolescence in some children are the symptoms of the first cry-outs from the Spirit.

Although Spirit is pressed into the corner of the heart, he always tries to knock on the door and shouts out to the mind who has taken charge in the body's deeds, the mind is so 'confident' that he is doing the 'right' thing and he never listens again. With time accumulated, Spirit is totally forgotten by the mind.

In reality the Spiritual realm and the physical realm are overlapping instead of parallel. All beings have a preferential realm to live in these two worlds according to its vibrational frequency – the higher frequency of energy a being resonates with, the more expanded consciousness and awareness of all existence in the universe can the being harness till the two worlds merge into Oneness (Wuji) completely in the Mind Eye, and this is the Consciousness of God.

Look at the Taichi Symbol again in figure 1#, meditate on it till you can see white behind the black, and black behind the white.

In God Consciousness there is no judgment, no white and black, right and wrong, good and evil, there is no separation, everything connects to everything else, everything is interwoven together, and everything becomes One, Pure Existence. In human's perspective God Consciousness is perceived as Unconditional Love, the sense of Equality and Freedom, and these are encoded in each being's DNA when they are born into this physical world as the Law of God – you do not have to be somebody or to do something to receive Unconditional Love and freedom. If you are demanded or have to do anything out of fear without your willingness, to receive something or a 'promise', that request is not from Love but bargain. Then you can be sure that is not from the True Oneness God, instead someone who bears the traits of the world and flesh.

According to the locality of each being in this Two in One reality, we know there are demigods, like the ones in myths called deities, gods who are assigned responsibilities by Oneness God for different life necessities, who have power but still are on the journey for achieving Freedom and Liberation.

Bhagavad Gita 3.10-12,

In the beginning of creation, the Lord of all creatures sent forth generations of men and demigods, along with sacrifices for Vishnu, and blessed them by saying, "Be thou happy by this yajna [sacrifice] because its performance will bestow upon you everything desirable for living happily and achieving liberation." The demigods, being pleased by sacrifices, will also please you, and thus, by cooperation between men and demigods, prosperity will reign for all. In charge of the various necessities of life, the demigods, being satisfied by the performance of yajna [sacrifice], will supply all necessities to you.

Neither the hosts of demigods nor the great sages know My origin or opulence, for, in every respect, I am the source of the demigods and sages.

So if a demigod or anyone does anything violating the Law of God, the Oneness God will not approve what he does. Without God's approval nothing can be fulfilled.

Traits of a demigod and flesh being demonstrated in rest of Genesis and Exodus.

Demigods in ancient scriptures were those gods, deities that acquire worship, offerings; Because they are also created beings, they have Yin Yang energy in them. Therefore they have similar limitations as humans do. If they are not pleased, they feel jealous, angry, they take revenge, they are dividers in people, place favors on individuals that invoking separation, crimes in Humankind, they play wrath on those who make mistakes, invoke

70

weakness (they call 'sins') in human flesh. All these traits belong to humans, however demigods possess much power than humans, therefore they stir up fears in human society in order to acquire their 'chosen people' to consume them and to show their own 'glory'

After Son of God slipped to duality world, this Yang energy 'Lord God' started to curse the serpent, the woman and man, and delivered his punishment to them. And out of fear and jealousy, and desires of showing his glory and magic power, 'Lord God' placed a series of events on vengeance that emitted immense negative energy hovering around Humankind.

I can easily list several dozens of events and occasions described in Genesis and Oxodus that represent these negative influences, but I need to avoid them to restrain from spreading the negativity. I myself would rather not read them more (except the first 3 chapters of Genesis) if I hadn't taken the assignment of writing this book. I had to spend hours even days on healing myself after reading them because it made my solar plexus pain. In order to trace the roots of today's issues in human society, I will need to take a few important cases for reflection:

These undesirable events are written in Genesis, so we would assume they are all first occurrences in human history:

Unfairness case by showing preference to one of Sons of God which invoked the first murder in human history – a story about Abel and Cain according to chapter 4, Genesis:

Now Abel was a keeper of sheep, and Cain a tiller of the ground. 3In the course of time Cain brought to the Lord an offering of the fruit of the ground, 4and Abel for his part brought of the firstlings of his flock, their fat portions. And the Lord had regard for Abel and his offering, 5but for Cain and his offering he had no regard. So Cain was very angry, and his countenance fell. … 8 Cain said to his brother Abel, 'Let us go out to the field.' And when they were in the field, Cain rose up against his brother Abel and killed him.

If the Lord is God, how could he favor one son disregard the other, in seeing both of whom brought him offerings from their work? Do you feel that is fair and equal? Some may say because Cain did not offer his best or first from his work, - then, that immediately removes the Lord from God's Consciousness because God does not place difference on good and bad, first or last. And just simply think if your father does this to you and your sibling, how do you feel and react?

Two earliest cases of lies and betrayals from Abraham and Issac

1st case, Chapter 12

10 Now there was a famine in the land. So Abram went down to Egypt to reside there as an alien, for the famine was severe in the land.11When he was about to enter Egypt, he said to his wife Sarai, 'I know well that you are a woman beautiful in appearance; 12and when the Egyptians see you, they will say, "This is his wife"; then they will kill me, but they will let you live. 13Say you are my sister, so that it may go well with me because of you, and that my life may be spared on your account.' 14When Abram entered Egypt the Egyptians saw that the woman was very beautiful. 15When the officials of Pharaoh saw her, they praised her to Pharaoh. And the woman was taken into Pharaoh's house. 16And for her sake he dealt well with Abram; and he had sheep, oxen, male donkeys, male and female slaves, female donkeys, and camels. 17 But the Lord afflicted Pharaoh and his house with great plagues because of Sarai, Abram's wife. 18So Pharaoh called Abram, and said, 'What is this you have done to me? Why did you not tell me that she was your wife? 19Why did you say, "She is my sister", so that I took her for my wife? Now then, here is your wife; take her, and be gone.' 20And Pharaoh gave his men orders concerning him; and they set him on the way, with his wife and all that he had.

2nd case, chapter 26

6 So Isaac settled in Gerar. 7When the men of the place asked him about his wife, he said, 'She is my sister'; for

he was afraid to say, 'My wife,' thinking, 'or else the men of the place might kill me for the sake of Rebekah, because she is attractive in appearance.' 8When Isaac had been there a long time, King Abimelech of the Philistines looked out of a window and saw him fondling his wife Rebekah. 9So Abimelech called for Isaac, and said, 'So she is your wife! Why then did you say, "She is my sister"?' Isaac said to him, 'Because I thought I might die because of her.' 10Abimelech said, 'What is this you have done to us? One of the people might easily have lain with your wife, and you would have brought guilt upon us.' 11So Abimelech warned all the people, saying, 'Whoever touches this man or his wife shall be put to death.'

Imagine if an adult human, who has never read or heard of Bible, is given these two paragraphs to read, what would be his reaction or sentiment towards Abraham and Issac? Probably both of them would be cursed as busters who lied and 'sold' or intended to sell their own wife to save their own life and get prosperous from it. Alas, how can you believe the two important men from the bloodline as 'chosen people' by 'God' told lies and became so demoralized to betray their own wife who were chosen by God as their life companion? Even worse, 'the Lord' if did not have God's standard, how couldn't he even keep a human standard by giving these two men punishment or just warning them to show his 'righteousness'? The Lord not only freed them from blaming, but instead he punished the innocents who did not know the truth *'the Lord afflicted Pharaoh and his house with great plagues'.* What a twisted image it was placed on human's mind! Have you ever heard a saying 'the innocent won't get blamed'?

So what was the Lord's standard? Were these the perfect examples for today's similar lies, betrayals among some family life? Were these the 'inspirations' for today's films, TV series featuring family plots? If you ask people whether or not they favour this kind of lies and betrayals, probably most of them would say 'No' consciously, but at subconscious level they may think it is natural, it is human's nature because even Bible has the stories to prove them. Does a baby human being know what a lie is when he comes into this world? Is he a sinner when comes into this world? What a shame!

Possession of material wealth is the root for separation of kindred, from which derived early conflicts, fights and burdens of complicated rules and laws among human society, and further set forth on the track for wars

Chapter13

2 Now Abram was very rich in livestock, in silver, and in gold. 3He journeyed on by stages from the Negeb as far as Bethel, to the place where his tent had been at the beginning, between Bethel and Ai, 4to the place where he had made an altar at the first; and there Abram called

on the name of the Lord. 5Now Lot, who went with Abram, also had flocks and herds and tents, 6so that the land could not support both of them living together; for their possessions were so great that they could not live together, 7and there was strife between the herders of Abram's livestock and the herders of Lot's livestock. At that time the Canaanites and the Perizzites lived in the land.

8 Then Abram said to Lot, 'Let there be no strife between you and me, and between your herders and my herders; for we are kindred. 9Is not the whole land before you? Separate yourself from me. If you take the left hand, then I will go to the right; or if you take the right hand, then I will go to the left.' 10Lot looked about him, and saw that the plain of the Jordan was well watered everywhere like the garden of the Lord, like the land of Egypt, in the direction of Zoar; this was before the Lordhad destroyed Sodom and Gomorrah. 11So Lot chose for himself all the plain of the Jordan, and Lot journeyed eastwards; thus they separated from each other. 12Abram settled in the land of Canaan, while Lot settled among the cities of the Plain and moved his tent as far as Sodom. 13Now the people of Sodom were wicked, great sinners against the Lord.

After Lot moved in the cities in the plain and Sodom, probably their behaviors stirred up sentiments among the locals, so the local people came to seize their house while the angels appeared in their house:

Chapter 19

"4 … the men of the city, the men of Sodom, both young and old, all the people to the last man, surrounded the house; 5and they called to Lot, 'Where are the men who came to you tonight? Bring them out to us, so that we may know them.' 9 … 'This fellow came here as an alien, and he would play the judge! Now we will deal worse with you than with them.' "

When wars were fought in the Valley of Siddim of Sodom and Gomorrah, Abraham was forced to involve himself to fight:

Chapter 14

12they also took Lot, the son of Abram's brother, who lived in Sodom, and his goods, and departed. 14When Abram heard that his nephew had been taken captive, he led forth his trained men, born in his house, three hundred and eighteen of them, and went in pursuit as far as Dan.

Abraham and his nephew Lot were living together when they first left their father's home for the land of Cannan. By the time they reached Bethel they had so much extra livestock plus silver and gold (who gave them the idea of possessing silver and gold, and how did they know gold and silver had more value? The most important - when were gold and silver used in common? It seems only around 600-500 BCE they were common in possession as currency), so the land they were living on was no longer big enough to support both of them living together, they had to separate, and one of them had to leave for another land and therefore resulted in conflicts with local inhabitants. Did they really need so much extra belongs?

You all have or know the experience that no matter how big your house is, if you gather stuff up not in use, very soon you will fill up your entire house and if you are reluctant to get rid of them nor get detached from them, you will feel and truly be burdened because all of those stuff cost your time and energy to keep in order. How did Abraham start on this road?

It was led by his own ambition - the over-heated Yang energy, because Abraham wanted to be a great man leading a great nation surpassing his brothers and have a lot of possessions. So the Lord (mistaken by him as God) appeared to him and laid him his 'promise', and the Lord also input the concept 'enemy' into his mind as cursers:

Chapter 12

Now the Lord said to Abram, 'Go from your country and your kindred and your father's house to the land that I will show you.2I will make of you a great nation, and I will bless you, and make your name great, so that you will be a blessing. 3I will bless those who bless you, and the one who curses you I will curse; and in you all the families of the earth shall be blessed.' And they set forth to go to the land of Canaan. When they had come to the land of Canaan, 6Abram passed through the land to the place at Shechem, to the oak of Moreh. At that time the Canaanites were in the land.

7Then the Lord appeared to Abram, and said, 'To your offspring I will give this land.' So he built there an altar to the Lord, who had appeared to him. 8From there he moved on to the hill country on the east of Bethel, and pitched his tent, with Bethel on the west and Ai on the east; and there he built an altar to the Lord and invoked the name of the Lord. 9And Abram journeyed on by stages towards the Negeb.

14The Lord said to Abram, after Lot had separated from him, 'Raise your eyes now, and look from the place where you are, northwards and southwards and eastwards and westwards; 15for all the land that you see I will give to you and to your offspring for ever. 16I will make your offspring like the dust of the earth; so that if one can count the dust of the earth, your offspring also can be counted. 17Rise up, walk through the length and the breadth of the land, for I will give it to you.'

In Chapter 15, it could not be much clearer than the following that shows the ill relationship between Abraham and the Lord. It seems that as long as someone obeyed and believed him, the Lord would regard him as 'righteousness':

6And he believed the Lord; and the Lord reckoned it to him as righteousness.

7 Then he said to him, 'I am the Lord who brought you from Ur of the Chaldeans, to give you this land to possess.' 8But he said, 'O Lord God, how am I to know that I shall possess it?' ...

17 When the sun had gone down and it was dark, a smoking fire-pot and a flaming torch passed between these pieces. 18On that day the Lord made a covenant with Abram, saying, 'To your descendants I give this land, from the river of Egypt to the great river, the river Euphrates,19the land of the Kenites, the Kenizzites, the Kadmonites, 20the Hittites, the Perizzites, the Rephaim, 21the Amorites, the Canaanites, the Girgashites, and the Jebusites.'

So led by the Lord who gave Abraham big 'promise' as he liked for the exchange of Abraham's offerings - building altars for him, from then on, generations after generations until today Abraham's offspring have been piously fighting for the land that the Lord 'promised' to them because they believed the Lord was God, and they were the 'chosen people' who had and have the 'privilege' to take over the 'God-given' land from their brothers and sisters. Oh, the offspring of Abraham, I Love you! But pleeease wake up now, for the sake of yourself and your kindred! You are forgiven already! You are healed already! God Bless you!

Because You have been blinded by your own desires and created the illusions of 'promise' from the Lord or your own mind, and you have not awaken even after the 'promise' had been kept broken many times already from one side by the Lord through the famines fell on the land of Canaan during Abraham, Issac, Jacob and in Egypt where Moses resided. Look at chapter 26, Genesis, The Lord simply repeated the same to each of them he said to Abraham the following and it is only because Abraham obeyed him and kept his Statues:

'2The Lord appeared to Isaac and said, 'Do not go down to Egypt; settle in the land that I shall show you. 3Reside in this land as an alien, and I will be with you, and will bless you; for to you and to your descendants I will give all these lands, and I will fulfill the oath that I swore to your father Abraham. 4I will make your offspring as numerous as the stars of heaven, and will give to your offspring all these lands; and all the nations of the earth shall gain blessing for themselves through your offspring, 5because Abraham obeyed my voice and kept my charge, my commandments, my statutes, and my laws.'

Were those 'promises of blessing and thriving' to your offspring and other nations through your offspring supposed to be famines? Still do not believe all these were illusions?

Then the Lord revealed himself to Moses that he was not God, his name was 'the Lord' in chapter 6, Exodus, but Moses failed in recognizing this:

'2 God also spoke to Moses and said to him: 'I am the Lord. 3I appeared to Abraham, Isaac, and Jacob as God Almighty, but by my name "The Lord", I did not make myself known to them. 4I also established my covenant with them, to give them the land of Canaan, the land in which they resided as aliens.'

Most people believe the first five books of Old Testament originated from Moses, and if that is the case, it is not so difficult to understand why all the patriarchic figures went astray led by the Lord, a demigod who had full of flesh traits and was conditioned to the duality world, because Moses' mind was overwhelmed by a single Yang force energy which blinded his eye to see.

Two major severe consequences in humanity if the story lines in Genesis and Exodus are taken as the main events in the creation of humankind

-    No1# It implanted the concept of 'chosen people' in human's mind which has induced in some people the sense of superiority to 'non-chosen people', which led these 'chosen people' start immediately, as described in Genesis and Exodus, and in later history, to go out of their own land to grab from other people in the name of 'God's mission', as showed in history the major European countries to discover the new world and to colonize in Asia, Africa and Americas. As a consequence it sewed a seed for bitter fruits among the humanity, therefore having fulfilled the 'prophecies' of retribution, with the slaughter of six million Jews in WWII as a climax event. Why retribution events were predicted in prophecies? Because the Lord knew the Law of God – the principles of Equality, Freedom and Unconditional Love. Whenever these principles are trampled, retribution has to be paid no matter in what space time!

- No2# Event after event around all kinds of crimes described in the two books deeply and effectively implanted a sense of guilt as sinners, an ill conception in the originally innocent minds of all human beings, which has easily made human beings at bay, plus the fear of wraths falling from 'God', to accept all kinds of complicated commandments and judgments, and from then on human beings would carry on these heavy burdens and never raise their heads and straighten their backs. All the demoralization accounts in the two books generate very negative influence, deeply damaged the image of humanity who were created in the image of God, i.e. it damaged the self-esteem, self-confidence of people who have been following the religion, deprived them of the ability to recognize themselves. As Mahatma Gandhi ever said "You must not lose faith in humanity. Humanity is an ocean; if a few drops of the ocean are dirty, the ocean does not become dirty".

Here is a dialogue between a spiritual master and his disciples, it may be appropriate for you to ponder on:

<They saw> a Samaritan carrying a lamb on his way to Judea. He (the spiritual master) said to his disciples, "(Why *does) that man (carry) the lamb around?*"

They said to him, "So that he may kill it and eat it."

He said to them, "While it is alive, he will not eat it, but only when he has killed it and it has become a corpse."

They said to him, "He cannot do so otherwise."

He said to them, "You too, look for a place for yourself within the Repose, lest you become a corpse and be eaten."

These lines are from verse 60, Gospel of Thomas. The spiritual master was Jesus. Sometimes Jesus' words may seem quite sharp to some people, but they are pinpointing.

And the whole teaching of Jesus Christ was completely different from the Old Testament. In verse 3, Gospel of Thomas:

"... When you come to know yourselves, then you will become known, and you will realize that it is you who are the sons of the living Father. But if you will not know yourselves, you dwell in poverty and it is you who are that poverty."

Yes, It is true, you have all the resources in your soul that dwells in your heart, and it was given to you on the day, even before the day when you were born into this physical world; but your innocent mind was poisoned by these irreligious teaching and your mind started adding all kinds of reasons and arguments to put up layer after layer of walls and bars and locks that buried deeply away the treasure you inherited from your Living Father so that you feel so powerless and hopeless; therefore 'you dwell in poverty and it is you who are that poverty'. Nowadays there is nearly one third of the world population, if not every Sunday, very frequently listen to these untrue teaching and very damaging preaches. No wonder there are so much confusions around the world which, I see, are part of the sources for many undesirable actions and reactions, conflicts and struggles.

Oh, my Brothers and Sisters, if you truly want to know about God, read Gospel of Thomas, and those are the raw sayings from Jesus Christ, without any added narration or cutting-offs, and they are not tainted by ignorant or ill minds; if you really want to know about yourself and your relationship with God, want to know about the Ultimate Truth, read Bhagavad Gita, which contains the most enlightened messages from the Divine, in my opinion. And when you read them, go to a quiet place by yourself, focus your eyes on the scriptures and your mind on the Absolute Truth, meditate and pray, ask God for wisdom and let you understand the true meanings!

At Global Domain, Yang energy over took Yin energy resulting in prevalence of countries in the west over the eastern and other non-western countries

If the whole human society, or the human species is viewed as one living being, then sustaining an overall healthy population of the species is the purpose of its life, as all other species do if you observe; the individual human activities plus regional groups of individual activities is the driving Yang force for humanity moving forward, and the longing for stability, peace in human's hearts is the Yin force at the opposite; then the principals of Equality, Freedom and Unconditional love are of the Law to hold these two forces in One Union. There is one difference between human species and other species, that is you have been given by God the 'privilege' of responsibility or 'right' to manage the full circle of lives on Earth, including yourselves.

All other species, no matter they are animals, plants or

any other organisms, seem following some kinds of natural laws to take birth, grow and die, to move around or not to move around to fulfill their life cycles. Remember they are also created by God. With God's creation, they have Spirit in them and quite clearly they are living in that Spirit much more than humans do. They know how and where to migrate thousands of miles following season's change; they know instinctively how to be a block on the full circle of lives, everything that goes in and comes out of them are in the circle; they mourn on life losses of their group members but not attached to it by building tombs and memorials for the dead; they even develop feelings towards members of other species and help them to survive; they help raise the youngsters in their social group. Even when new leader males take over from other groups of their kind, in the case of lion's life, it is just for reproduction (life evolving) purpose and for this privilege they take on an enormous responsibility for protecting their pride at the risk of losing their lives. It is so awesome, animal Spirit! They all just follow the natural laws!

As human beings already took on their astray journey after they slipped into the duality state world and disconnected with Spirit, led by the over-played Yang force; throughout the whole middle ages, the earth was subdivided by regions habited by locals who had variants in philosophies and religions. Most of the regional groups were in feudal or imperial social structures where there was one iconic figure that was the authority to control all aspects of social life. In Europe the influence of catholic Monarchs and Christianity was prevalent in the society while in Asia Confucianism, Buddhism, Taoism, Hinduism, Islamism etc. were adopted in different areas; plus indigenous practices in Africa and Americas

The countries in Europe powered by the Christianity ideals, pioneered by some individuals to spread the religion to the world by exploring other parts of the world plus the driving force of economic interests, started the colonization to Americas, Asia and Africa.

Interestingly, all of the three main explorers sent by Portugal or Spain were Christian who had or were given the mission of spreading the religion, Leif Ericson (11th century), Dom Vasco da Gama (15th-16th century) and Christopher Columbus (15th century), especially the later who was piously believed that he was playing an active role in God's mission in spreading Christianity to the New World. A description in Wikipedia wrote (modified on June 4, 2014): *Under the auspices of the Catholic Monarchs of Spain, he completed four voyages across the Atlantic Ocean that led to general European awareness of the American continents. Those voyages, and his efforts to establish permanent settlements on the island of Hispaniola, initiated the Spanish colonization of the New World.*

Some blame Columbus for his discovery of the New World that led to the Spanish colonization of it. Well, finding a new world was not a bad thing, it was just simply an event in life, but what the next actions were important.

It is normal in life evolution for any living beings to experience new life if the exploration voyages are viewed as the Yang force in play, however all Yang force activities need to be balanced with the Yin force in order to have a healthy humanity society, and the governing law is the invisible but the True Law of God which is written on every human's heart, i.e. the Law of Equality, Freedom, Unconditional Love; since human beings had had Spirit locked deeply in the corner of their hearts long time ago, they could not hear the call of the Spirit, instead pushing only by their own desires, therefore they lost their minds and sights, and did not know at what point they should have stopped or restrained their actions.

And then also energized by the liberation of individual human minds from the two Renaissances through 12th - 17th century and the French revolution in late 18th century, which profoundly affected Europe and modern history, marking the decline of powerful monarchies and churches and a leap of mind liberation of individuals with the rise of democracy and nationalism, and also fueled by the nearly 100 years of industrial revolution later in 18th-19th century, the European countries started expanding at a full spring to the world through colonization from 15th to early 20th century.

While other parts of the globe on the contrary during

those periods still remained in the state of feudal imperial social schemes with a much more closed, still mind, or in a remote indigenous tribal societies. Take China and Asia for example, the societies were totally controlled by feudal imperial authorities and its applied philosophies for governing were Confucianism plus Taoism in China, Hinduism in India, from which the governing class placed much emphasis on traditions, rituals and harmonies to the society while individuals with governing authority bearing much Yang-tilted energy in themselves, and this formed a complex social structures, which played an active role in the repression of the Yang force energy expression at individual levels as a whole in the Asian society. In China, the overly-emphasized harmonious effect can be attributed to the misinterpretation of Taoist philosophy throughout centuries to which the governing authorities consulted and whose essence was the principles of inaction in governing and Yin-Yang balance for governing individuals in their actions, however, they have been applied by the governing individuals mainly onto the people except to themselves; as a consequence, the ambitions of governing individuals took in control and over-restrained the expression of Yang-force in individuals of the society. This might have been the deep root for the two similar devastating events towards intellectuals and culture inheritance, namely the Burning Books and Burying Scholars in Qin Dynasty (221-206BCE) and the Culture Revolution in the People's Republic of China; particularly the one in Qin dynasty that caused an immense and irretrievable loss in the history records of one of the earliest human civilizations in terms of creation myths, earlier culture and philosophies! Oh God, whenever this episode is mentioned, my heart aches! Everyone who studies TaoTeJing needs to take heed on Chapter 3.4

是以圣人之治，虚其心，实其腹，弱其志，强其骨。A Saint in governing would humble his heart, enrich his belly (with the knowledge of Tao, i.e. Laws of Heaven, Laws of Nature), weaken his ambitions and strengthen his body'.

While for thousands of years, this verse has been misinterpreted, because of one word difference, as for imposing on the masses, which is contradictory to Laozi's essence of philosophy.

And therefore at a collective level the whole Asia was over played by the Yin energy, which was a sharp contrast in the face of an overly Yang force charged European countries. Asia had one country as an exception without Yin energy overplayed, that was Japan which took a social reform in the mid of 19th century known as Meiji Restoration, which again was an example of Yang force overplay: After the mind restriction was lifted with the social reform, immediately Japan started its colonial expansion in Asia till the end of WWII.

Were there ever other possible roads for the human species to move forward up till now after they slipped into their duality state of world? Have you ever heard of the saying: Every road gets to Rome?

Achieve the balance of Yin-Yang energy by knowing more about your body and moving beyond the physics

If life is the ocean, your body is the ship to carry you to your life destiny, then your mind is the captain, your soul is the compass.

For better understanding the answers to the above question, and get prepared for moving to the next section, you will need to know more about your physical body, which you have heard from nowhere else before:

As you already knew through the text of early sessions, you are a spiritual being crystallized in your physical body in this physical world by the seed of Divine energy, and after you came to this world, you started to be subject to the conditions of the material nature which are difficult to overcome. So gradually the Spirit, Self, was left behind and locked in a corner of your heart. Your mind and the senses of your body constantly interact with the lower vibrational energy of the material world in forms of people, events; and with these complex energies in play, your mind is bewildered. To make yourself feel comfortable, your mind wants to take control on what is happening around you; in time he completely forgets about your soul, the Spirit; but of course he cannot control everything, all his struggles are just blind actions and reactions on a habitual track because of the law of action and reaction in the physical world (Third Law of Newton) in play, and he falls into the three modes of material nature: Goodness, Passion and Ignorance.

According to Bhagavad Gita, Goodness, Passion and Ignorance are the three modes of the material nature. Every manifested beings are bounded to activities according to the three modes.

The mode of goodness, purer than the others, is illuminating; operating at the highest vibration of the material world and it frees one from all blind action and reactions. People who are in the mode of goodness have a strong feeling of connection to all beings, they feel the happiness when others are happy, they feel the pain when others pain, they know what others do not know and have full of compassion. They are not indifferent, although aware of everything, good or bad, glory or humiliation, but not disturbed by them; they do not renounce actions, but renounce fruition results from actions, because they understand that they do not cause the results, they only perform prescribed duties, they know that the results of their actions depend on a lot of factors, which are out of their own will, and ultimately are in the hands of the Divine. They do not feel unhappy when results are out of expectation, they do not refuse when fruits come from their prescribed duty. So people who are situated in the mode of goodness always have a sense of happiness and knowledge; and real knowledge develops with the expansion of their consciousness, their soul is in charge of their activities.

The mode of passion is born of excessive desires and longings, which are attached to fruition results; when people are locked in the mode of passion, great attachment, fruition activities, intense endeavors and uncontrollable desires and hankering develop; strong desires for money, for material wealth, for power, for fame, for expected results, for success etc. From the mode of passion, greed develops; when the mind is covered by greed, they would resort to any actions they can to strive to the results. They let their mind take full control of their deeds, they can only taste misery; in the case of individuals in power, destructive actions are taken, and they move into the mode of darkness.

The mode of darkness, born of ignorance, is the delusion of the mind, operating at the lowest level of vibration in the material world. The results of this mode are madness, indolence and sleep. People who are in the mode of ignorance are isolated from the feelings of other beings. Actions taken by these people are of foolishness, madness and illusion, to the extreme of abhorrent activities.

These three modes of the material natures are constantly in competition for supremacy in one individual and in the whole human society. That is why you see the fluctuations of morality in human society in different period of times.

The mode of Goodness is the purest and the most desirable state – the enlightened kingdom that human beings want to achieve and enter. And in form of energy, it constitutes the highest vibrational frequency in the three modes of the material world. If you let your mind in control of your actions, you are forever in the battle of the three modes, and most easily situated in the lower two modes because of the Law of Inertia and Gravitation; Only when you go beyond the physics, let your soul, the Spirit take full charge of your activities, in other words you let the soul be your compass, and follow your heart, each of you can gradually moves up to higher modes, and even beyond the three modes of material world.

The development of the Chinese word '我' (English: I) reveals a process of human's unconscious mind guided by the Divine Conscious Mind, and it conveys the Divine message that:

I, the self, the body, is a field of battles if handled by the mind; however at the union with the Heaven Dog, a Chinese mythical animal recorded in Classic of Mountains and Seas 山海经, it can transform to the capitalized I, Self.

See fig 10

Oracle	Inscription	Qin Zhuan	Han LI

earliest	before Qin	from Qin	from Han

These are four versions of the Chinese word 'I' developed from oracle times till the modern days. On the right side of each version of the word, it is an ancient weapon representing 'battle' or 'struggle'; the left side from the two earliest versions was a 'hand', a part of the body, but from Qin dynasty (206-221BCE), after the first Emperor Qin united the Middle Kingdom, the writing system was also united and simplified. So the left side of '我'

became '犬 '(English: dog) radicalized as '犭 ' plus a stroke at the top representing 'heaven', thus the left side became Heaven Dog. According to Classic of Mountains and Seas, there was a heaven dog coming out from flood water, its body looked like a fox with white on its head, and it could ward off anything ominous. The Heaven Dog had divine nature and had power to guard the flesh body, so it is a spirit.

Do you say it is a coincidence that people have also recognized that the English word 'DOG' is 'GOD' if written backward? And how did dogs evolve to be human's companions and loyal friends in history? Is it also a Divine intention that has laid a profound meaning for humankind? Isn't that fascinating?!

Now please come back! Your soul, the Spirit comes from the Super Soul, the Supreme Spirit, God, the Infinity, which is beyond, transcendental to all the material natures; its light dissolves all material darkness. When you let your soul, the Spirit guide you, the Yin-Yang energy inside you would be kept towards balance, because your soul always knows when and where the Yin energy needs more charge, also knows when and where it is time for the Yang energy to take more charge. From then on, you will embark on the journey to make the divine reunion of your body and Spirit, mind and Soul, the outside and the inside, and happiness will start to be your companion on the journey; even before the two merge completely into One which is of nonduality, you enter the mode of goodness of the material nature. If more people in human society enter the state of goodness, the Kingdom of Heaven would be manifest on the earth.

The good news: It is not far ... I see thousands and millions of souls are wakening, they are spreading the good news upon the earth; the light is already within each of you, you just need to make the decision to let it be ignited!

Those who are waiting for Messiah to come again to save you, I say to you: He only saves those who want to save themselves! If you do not do the work and get prepared, even if He stands in front of you, you cannot recognize

Him.

As Jesus said: *"Recognize what is before your face and that which is hidden from you will be revealed to you. For there is nothing hidden which shall not be made manifest, nor buried which shall not be raised."*

There are several verses in which Jesus refers to the Two in One energy, and urges you to emerge the flesh and the Spirit into One. To check them yourself, look at Verses 11#, 22#, 30#, 48#, 61#, 106# etc. in Gospel of Thomas. Here is verse 48#

Jesus said, *"If two (mind and soul or flesh and spirit) make peace with each other in this one house (the body), they will say to the mountain, 'Move Away,' and it will move away."*

Soul Awakening Meditation

Before you start the meditation, read the following guidance several times till you remember the process, then quiet yourself, to start.

Close your eyes, breathe slowly and deeply, in and out ...

Imagine yourself become a small figure looking at your own body. Now gently enter into your body from the chest. Along the corridor coming to a transparent room, from the window of the room you see many rooms one inside another with doors and windows, each one with a lock on its door; at a corner of the inner room, you see a little figure squatting, looking towards the window. When the eyes of you two meet, you suddenly realize, the little figure is you; all of a sudden you are overwhelmed by emotions with tears running down. Without any hesitation, with all your might you rush to the door and break it, and one by one you break all the doors open; when you get in, the little figure stands right in front of you waiting for you, you hold the little figure in your arms, and say the following words:

I am sorry! Pride, fear or ignorance, if because of any reasons I locked you down in that corner, please forgive me! I love you! Please, in God's name, help me clear them away, and help me reconnect with the Creator, help me find my true purpose in life!

Upon your words, you feel a stream of warmth flowing from your heart to your whole body, and the little figure instantly merged into your heart; at the moment rays of crystal golden lights from your heart shooting out and shimmering and sparkling, the lights glowing and filling your whole body and your whole aura; upon your looking at the ruins of the transparent rooms you just torn down, they are immediately dissolved by the golden lights from your heart.

Now slowly walk back along the corridor, come out gently from your chest and seal the little opening on it; looking around, you are surrounded by a vast land of green grass with flowers blooming and animals capering. It is a sunny day, and a peaceful melody floating into your ears… enjoy as long as you wish… then take three deep breaths.

When you are ready, open your eyes.

This is a powerful guided meditation; it can help free you from old bondages, attachments, let you start feeling the murmuring of your heart. And it is a start for you to reconnect to the Spirit. You can do this meditation frequently whenever you feel falling back to your old habit of thinking or doing things.

Today's Money driven social scheme originated from the possession system, developed and spread to the whole world in acceleration by the unbalanced Yin-Yang force energy, but not without reasons

To add to his possessions, Abraham promoted commercial trade by turning down two simple and sincere free offers of land from the Hittites after his wife Sarah died:

Chapter 23, Genesis

3Abraham rose up from beside his dead, and said to the Hittites, 4'I am a stranger and an alien residing among you; give me property among you for a burying-place, so that I may bury my dead out of my sight.' 5The Hittites answered Abraham, 6'Hear us, my lord; you are a mighty prince among us. Bury your dead in the choicest of our burial places; none of us will withhold from you any burial ground for burying your dead.'

7Abraham rose and bowed to the Hittites, the people of the land. 8He said to them, 'If you are willing that I should bury my dead out of my sight, hear me, and entreat for me Ephron son of Zohar, 9so that he may give me the cave of Machpelah, which he owns; it is at the end of his field. For the full price let him give it to me in your presence as a possession for a burying-place.' 10Now Ephron was sitting among the Hittites; and Ephron the Hittite answered Abraham in the hearing of the Hittites, of all who went in at the gate of his city,11'No, my lord, hear me; I give you the field, and I give you the cave that is in it; in the presence of my people I give it to you; bury your dead.' 12Then Abraham bowed down before the people of the land. 13He said to Ephron in the hearing of the people of the land, 'If you only will listen to me! I will give the price of the field; accept it from me, so that I may bury my dead there.' 14Ephron answered Abraham, 15'My lord, listen to me; a piece of land worth four hundred shekels of silver—what is that between you and me? Bury your dead.' 16Abraham agreed with Ephron; and Abraham weighed out for Ephron the silver that he had named in the hearing of the Hittites, four hundred shekels of silver, according to the weights current among the merchants.

Simplicity is the pure and beautiful nature of God Head; by going to the opposite it distracts people from worshiping God through focusing their minds on other complex things. Why did Abraham, the father of the 'chosen people' do this?

You all probably know at the beginning in human history nobody possessed anything, everyone roamed around laboring for their needs. When possession appeared, it led to trade, when trade appeared, it led to the use of currency, when currency appeared, it led to the conceptions of value and residue value, and when value and residue value occupied human's mind, it led to the conception of profit; after human's mind was consumed by profit, eventually the money driven scheme prevails the world till today in human society. The profit- and money-driven social scheme has driven human desires out of control, turn them into lusts. When lust arises, the mind gets deluded and bewildered, if a mind is under the control of delusion and bewilderment, it directs the body to doing everything without even awareness to the devastation of others as well as of himself.

Money driven social scheme accelerates after WWII in the unbalanced Yin-Yang energy world

With the colonization spreading all over the world, the full Yang energy charged social scheme - highly industrialized production and commercials have been brought to the world, and after WWII and with the decolonization, the colonial countries of Europe withdrew from most of the third worlds, but the money-driven scheme plus open-mind culture had been planted in the Yin energy dominated part of the world as social advancing seeds and later on grew into a full Yang force. Since then throughout decades at different degrees almost all countries in the world have gone into this money-driven scheme and it brought a big change materially for people's life. Just in the last 10 years the growth in global material wealth has risen by 68 percent to reach a new all-time high of $241 trillion with an average of $51,600 per adult. However this growth has been achieved at the sacrifice of something else much more valuable and creating serious problems that threaten the healthy development and advancement of humanity and the whole earth life by breaking the earth ecosystems through depletion of natural resources for regeneration of life supply, environmental pollution, uncontrolled population growth of human species, extinction of wildlife and the destruction of wildlife natural habitats both on land and in the ocean. Besides, the money-driven scheme drove people apart further from the Eternal Family, and *'the eternal family was destroyed, then womanhood of the family was polluted and unwanted population increase'* - Bhagavad Gita

No wonder some people feel so doomed about humanity, they worry humanity cannot jump out of the black hole. All circles of people in the world are so drawn to the money-driven scheme either by will or by force, or unaware of it - at the global domain, countries are trying to move up to the top of GDP list, competing who is the strongest to reach out into the outer space, whose stock market noses up; at sub and individual domains, everyone tries to surpass others in earning more money so as to either get themselves more things to possess, be it a car, a house, a name or just some basic life necessities; everyone eyes on the Forbes for its world wealth list each year so that they may be set as models for themselves to follow, even some direct mind training programs are focused on how to attract more money.

Who do you think the ruler of the world is? The president of the United States? The President of the People's Republic of China? or The Pope of Roman Catholic Church? No, none of them! It is money! Even these people have to be a servant of money, because without money they cannot truly move things around, get things seriously done! Who do you think the slaves are in the world? Those in some African countries or those labors at the lowest of the whole human society? Not exactly! In fact all of the people who are living in the reach of this modern world are!

As Jesus has already warned while He was on Earth. In verse 7, Gospel of Thomas:

"Blessed is the lion which becomes man when consumed by man; and cursed is the man whom the lion consumes, and the lion becomes man."

'the Lion' in the saying refers to lust, lust for money, lust for power, lust for sense pleasures; here in today's world collectively, it particularly refers to lust for money – man and money almost equals to each other, they consume each other, in the end money is blessed to thriving all over the world, while man suffers the consequences.

Thus the money-driven social scheme widens the gap between social classes further and further; it deprives people at the lower income end of their right to participate in mainstream activities in the society, and further deprives them of the right to enjoy a life of wellbeing; It funds on driving sons of men further away from Spirit, leading to further personal degradation; it also drives to pollute and exhaust the mother earth who gives and sustains the life of all living beings on it; And the whole world seems sucked in money swirls, no matter you come from the 10% of population who own the 86% material wealth or from the 2/3 of the adults who own 3% of it in the world. Fig 11 is the global material wealth diagram for 2013 by Credit Suisse.

Does it mean that in today's material abundance, 1% people in the world at the top of earning has the ability to enjoy exclusively 46% of it, while 90% people can only enjoy 14% of the material abundance for which they have

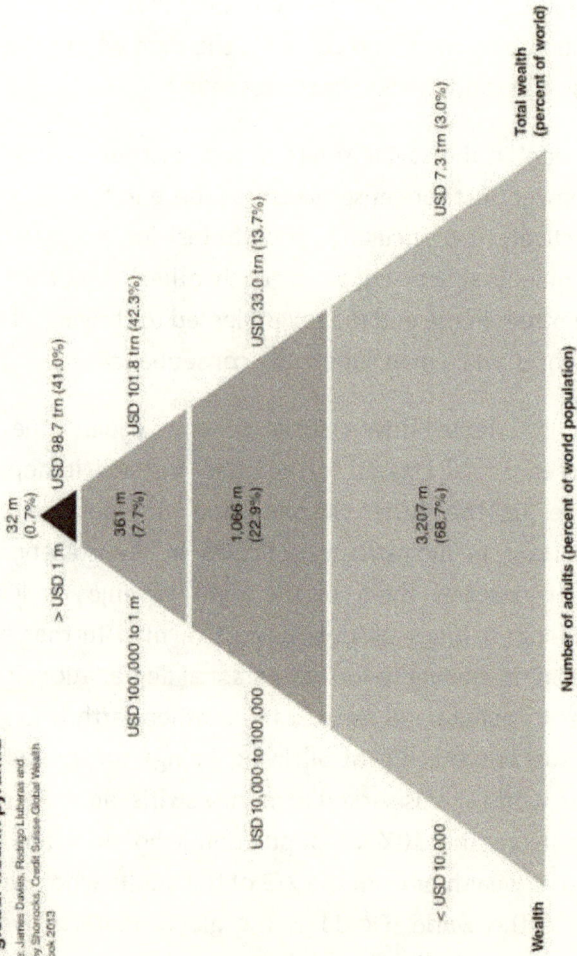

The global wealth pyramid

Source: James Davies, Rodrigo Lluberas and
Anthony Shorrocks, Credit Suisse Global Wealth
Databook 2013

> USD 1 m   32 m (0.7%)   USD 98.7 trm (41.0%)

USD 100,000 to 1 m   361 m (7.7%)   USD 101.8 trm (42.3%)

USD 10,000 to 100,000   1,066 m (22.9%)   USD 33.0 trm (13.7%)

< USD 10,000   3,207 m (68.7%)   USD 7.3 trm (3.0%)

Wealth   Number of adults (percent of world population)   Total wealth (percent of world)

Fig.11

106

labored? If all men are created equal, is this a system to deliver equality, fairness with nearly 69% world population being able to share only 3% of the world material abundance? Does it mean the 69% world population has lost their ability to work to exchange for a life of wellbeing or it is something else that has deprived them of their ability for the exchange?

While this book was written, one night in the early morning I had a dream, I saw an extravagant horse cart driving fast on a mountain road. There were holes on its canvass, and not far it was the cliff but hidden behind the trees so could not be seen; the horse had a lion head, there was not a driver, passengers in the cart were trying to block the holes from inside with anything they could get as they seemed trying to prevent strong winds going into the cart. As I woke up my heart felt so heavy and pained, but faintly I remember there seemed to be some sunlight over one side of the trees, so it made me feel better, hopeful.

My understanding of the dream is similar to the current situations in human society on Earth, it is obvious that mending the holes on the cart does not do any help, only by taking emergent actions or completely changing the course of the cart, the passengers on the cart can avoid falling off the cliff.

It was the renaissances and social reforms that have liberated the human minds which brought out the

ingenuity of humanity thus made the human society moving forward while money scheme mainly drives human's desires uncontrollable

Looking back the advancing history of human society, it was the continuous liberations of human minds through social reforms, renaissances that brought out the renovations in all aspects of the human society, be it in art, literature, science, philosophy, religion and social structures, within which religions and philosophies are the two most important aspects because they form human's belief systems which are the guidance of human's behaviors and activities. As mentioned in previous session, the Catholic Christianity was a dominion religion in Europe in the Middle Age through 15th century, immediately after the 12th century renaissance, Europe witnessed a radical and rapid change in the rate of innovations, new inventions in respect to managing means of production and economic growth. It also saw some major technological advances, including the invention of vertical windmills, spectacles mechanical clocks etc. And further and major leaps in all aspects of human society in Europe happened during and after the Renaissance, French Revolution, especially in religion and social structures. The dominion Catholic Monarch control of all social aspects was declined and divided by the reformation and arrival of New Protestant Christianity; The Declaration of the Rights of Man and of the Citizen, of August 1789, a fundamental document of the French Revolution, is the flagship in the history of human rights movements. It was the first time in history that recognized were the individuals as universal. From then on the modern world inventions arrive in a stream line. In the recent decades it has also been witnessed in other parts of the world. Whichever country adopted open-mind policies, its material production and supply would increase, such as China, Thailand etc.

The opposite proof of a major role that the liberation of human minds plays in social advancement is also China in its later period of the last dynasty Qing. While countries in Europe and its neighbor Japan actively took social reforms thus brought forth the leap in all aspects of the society and has gained advancing forces, the attempted Hundred Day's Reform of China failed due to its full-strength dominion Yin energy, therefore China remained in a feudal and semi-feudal, mind-isolated social structure for nearly another century totally lost its strength to advance.

Currency or money-driven scheme on the other hand is the major factor that pulls human's Yang energy out of control.

While money or currency is just an accounting tool to assist all the 'economic' activities, it does not create any true value on materials or production or services rendered, but to the opposite it creates an immense bubble, illusion of credit value based on speculation and overdraft of its real material production and service to be

109

rendered, and based on which some modern industries particularly financial related sectors have been created. These are the major driving forces, plus the conceptions of value and residue value playing in human's minds, like pouring gas on fire, they enflame endless human desires rocketing. As a result in collective human society, the Yin force is almost completely pressed down to the bottom as exemplified in the USA society. The main stream media take money-centered figures as their reporting focus, institutions also take money-related numbers as measurements for social progress, politics and religions have been corrupted by money, individual human minds are occupied by money even though there have been some cries with opposite voices but they are just like a glass of water pouring on a cart of burning wood – generates no effect at all.

So where is the Spirit, True Spirit in you, humankind, the One created in the image of God? It is not in you! For if it were, it would not have gone so far! If it were, you would have felt the feelings of others! If it were, you would have felt the feelings of the entire planet! Every Sunday you go to church, that does not guarantee you have Spirit in you; you worship a god, that does not guarantee you worship the Absolute Truth, *"If you do not fast as regards the world, you will not find the Kingdom. If you do not observe the Sabbath as a Sabbath, you will not see the Father."* Humans, Do you not to want to enter the Kingdom? Have you not sensed the urgency?

So many strong warnings and signals have been flashing in the last 200 years and in acceleration in the last a few decades – glacier melting, severe droughts and floods in different regions, extreme long cold and hot weather coexisting, the air being poisoned and becoming so filthy in big cities, big holes appearing in ozone layer, rivers and lakes have been poisoned, large ocean water dead zones swallowing sea lives, both animals on land and in waters have gone extinction and are being driven to extinction, frequent and large scale earthquake breaks and volcano eruptions, plus an explosive human population. The 9 magnitude earthquake happened in Japan in Mar 2011 already shifted the Earth's axis by about 6.5 inches which results in the change of the length of a day, the tilt of the earth, the speed of Earth rotation and the redistribution of the earth mass, which are surely further causing profound changes in Earth climate.

Look again at the historical dinosaur extinction event, perhaps it was forgivable if they were the reasons themselves to be driven to their own demise, because they had been living on Earth for nearly 200 million years, and they were not with God's image although they were created with God's Spirit, it might not have been a bad thing to have other forms of life evolve in; however human beings, you are only on Earth for couple of million years, you have not yet found out who you really are and where you will go after this life time, how can you just leave this world with this muddy mind? How can you let your offspring's future end in your hands in such a short space time? Did you forget you were created in the image of God? That means you are spiritual beings at the core and you have both Yin and Yang energies inside you to make peace to each other, that means you are the manager of your own body to make the two one. Wake up! Live out the Spirit of God, like those animals surrounding you, learn from them! You are the one lost sheep, no one else! Come back, God is calling! He still has not forgotten you! And this is your last chance!

Do you really still want to sit on this superficially extravagant, fast-moving cart that has already been torn thousands of hundreds of holes on it? Do you not recognize now it is urgent to take substantial actions and change the course? Everything has to move according to its Law, the Two-in-One Law; the Earth has to live its healthy life according to the same Two-in-One Law. If you do not change the course, nature will force in to take the last steps to rectify it, by then it is too late, no matter you are a billionaire or a beggar on street, you are a king or a shop assistant on Earth, the same consequences will fall. Everyone is equal in front of Nature, 'all men are created equal' as it is always quoted by a lot of you, but do you really understand its meaning? As Laozi said in his book of five thousand words, TaoTeJing:

"天地不仁，以万物为刍狗；圣人不仁，以百姓为刍狗 Heaven and Earth do not show mercy (by taking preference), they see all things pure and holy; A saint does *not show mercy (by taking preference), he sees all men pure and holy "*

Do Not Dismay, everything has been under the surveillance of Divine Vigilance. It is time to focus on solutions and make a conscious shift by abiding the Natural Laws in human activity, and living a balanced life in the Two Realities

If God has allowed it to go so far till today, then there must be something valuable from all the manifestations. You need to identify them and step on the valuables to move forward, gradually and completely cut off those which do not serve the society any more from both individuals and the human society.

Today's gross world production is estimated at US$87.43 trillion, which is the total world products and services produced by labor plus property supplied; while the world material wealth is reported at US$241 trillion which is the total earnings in US$ of the world population. What is the amount of the difference which takes up nearly 2/3 of world material wealth? Probably mainly money earned from mediate sectors, currency speculation sectors etc. And with the $87.43 trillion world products and services and houses supplied, the world probably already have more than enough for its need since sales reduction and waste can be seen everywhere and many people are bombarded by all kinds of sales information everyday.

The advancement of technology has made today's material supply and service means so abundant, and showed strong signs of more than enough for everyone, and it continues to be, provided the population is brought under control; and a lot in many aspects have been made wasted which is seen in people's everyday life:

Everyday you get so many mails in the form of letters, fliers, postcards, magazines for all kinds of product and service sales information from almost all industries; each year you also get a couple of thick phone books, most of the time you just directly throw them away because you use internet to get all those needed information. If someone vacations away for a month, he will probably get dozens of pounds of those mails piled up behind his door when he gets back. What a waste of the papers and the work done on it! Besides these, electronically you receive hundreds of spam mails for sales as well each day, 99.99% of them you may not want to receive at all; and everyone sees 'products on sales' everywhere at least at 50% cut. A lot of people may feel they are bombarded by this kind of sales information, but it seems nobody want to or can do anything about it productively, instead tolerate it, and in the end everyone does the same to everyone else in business. You can only see more effort and work have been put into creating anti-spam software, and reacted by much smarter spams; and there is an invisible war on the internet between spyware and antispyware, essentially most of them are actually around sales and blocking sales information, from which so much frustration arises from both sides and so many talents and energy have been wasted on these non-productive activities, but why do people still do that? because they want to earn money from it! Oh Humans, do you not recognize this old way of business does not work anymore? Do you think this is the life you should live on and would like to live on forever? If you do not want this happen to you, then why do you do this to others?! What a waste of everything! But are you aware that every piece of paper and prints on it you have wasted come from the blood of the Earth? Any energy you spent on producing these non-productive activities come from the blood of Earth. So for everything you take from the earth, have you ever asked yourself what you give it back?

Today's fast advancement in digital and web technology makes the world smaller and sets the trend for all human activities to have e-channels as its aids. The world internet users soon will be reaching 3 billion and will continue to grow. And this figure is obtained by only the statistics of unit computers connected to the internet, access from other e-devices and mobile devices not included. And in reality probably many of the individual users each own two or three e-equipments and e-devices, and after 2-4 years they resort to upgrade, and throw away the old ones. On one hand these equipments and devices come from resources on Earth, on the other hand these disposed e-wastes contain materials very toxic to the whole Earth environment which has already been severely polluted, some of them are not absorbable. Dare you imagine what kind of life you will be living if more individuals on Earth own these e-equipments and e-devices?

Today the availability and advancement of digital and web technology make well an abundant supply of material products and services in human's life. On top of that, they also paved the material foundation, making possible for humanity to enter the long dreamed and enlightened society, the Kingdom of God – a peaceful and beautiful garden with abundance of material supply, and with a river running to nurture the tree of life, citizens of the Kingdom have total equality, freedom to enjoy life, to feel unconditional love.

By making the world smaller, your spare time longer, life more convenient through making available all these technologies, God

- does not intend you to be more controlling, probing and competing to each other, but He wants you to be well connected to each other, become one people and return to the Eternal Family
- He does not intend you waste your talents by designing pointless programs and software or by playing endless hours of mind-killing games; but He intends you to use these technologies to

explore more of the unexplored world, the quantum energy world in particular
- He does not intend to make you farther away from Him; but He intends you to have more time to communicate with Him so as prepares you for the entering His Kingdom

To enter his Kingdom, you need to get prepared yourself for it, because in the Kingdom everything is run by the Laws of God – Equality, Freedom and Unconditional Love. No man-made laws can survive nor needed in the Kingdom nor allowed to be brought into it. All men need to work on and cut off their flesh traits before they can enter the Kingdom. For some it may be easier, it is achievable in this life time, for others it may take several lifetimes; it all depends on how much heart, effort and time you put in the work for the preparation. When each individual recognizes his flesh traits from which he can become detached thus live consciously and bring their new beliefs and behaviors into life, the whole humanity will be living with consciousness, and the human society will be in conscious movements and peace guided by the Two-in-One, One-in-Two Law.

There is not such a thing as business or personal life, social or private life, all activities, events are life experiences. Only when you make peace the outside with the inside, mind with soul, body with spirit, make the two One, then you can live a peaceful life; Only when you make peace with yourself, you can make peace with other people and the society; Only when you understand and know about yourself, you will know and understand about other living beings.

And these are the Truth! When you are in peace with yourself, you will start noticing and recognizing everything surround you, those that might look mysterious to you before may not do anymore, you seem empowered to face and solve any issues coming in your way, nothing is daunting anymore but simply new life experience, you start looking for helping others and the society that need help and see your actions as serving God's will and fulfilling your journey for the reunion of your body and spirit. Happiness and peace will start to accompany you all the way.

However to get there you will need to face yourself first and make deep and thorough retrospect, both on yourself and on the society as a collective one being, brave enough to admit and cut off those that become burdens and do not serve any more. To some you may have to experience a lot of pain, agony, but like the Phoenix Nirvana, you will need to experience the flame in order to shed away the old shell; to others this is a heavy extra download to your already wakened soul, and after you stand still with the power charged you may want to help other people and the society in the need; again for others this may make you feel bewildered, attempted to take undesirable actions, at this time go to the gym or to the mountains hiking to release yourself.

Let us do a Meditation and Prayer before moving on:

God/Supreme Spirit,

I believe I am part of You, please in Your Truth guide me in examining myself and the society which I am living in. I am brave, I am peaceful. I am open to face everything that comes out and needs to be removed. I trust Your Divine Omniscience and Your Intention for the goodness of all. I want to find solutions to the issues that are facing me and the entire humanity; I want to live a peaceful, harmonious and healthy life. Please help! Thank you for your listening! Amen!

The solutions and conscious shift

Yesterday morning when I woke up, God revealed to me the most shocking secret of secrets - about the twelve sons of Jacob (Israel) in Genesis 49. First I did not believe, I usually do not pay much attention to this part, believing they were just some trivial details, and quite often skipped this part. But He wanted me to read it again. When I read it again, it appeared to me that a lot of sacred sayings connect to each other, and they cannot make more sense than with this explanation of the twelve sons. More elaboration will be in Part Two of this writing. Here it needs to let you know that the 'Twelve Sons of Jacob' in Genesis 49 refer to some of human body's traits, desirable and undesirable in human's standard, but in God consciousness, a lot of them are not of tolerance and need to be removed. Here just list them and give explanation on the relevant ones. In the same order as mentioned in Chapter 49:

Reuben - Competitiveness

Simeon and Levi - anger and wrath

Judah - passion, desire, lust

Zebulun - stillness

Issachar - patience

Dan - judging

Gad - reacting

Ashe - gossiping

Naphtali - flattering

Joseph - faith

Benjamin - greed

Here are about Judah and Simon and Levi I need to give you now since they are relevant to this part of writing:

Original scripture -

49 Then Jacob called his sons, and said: 'Gather around,

that I may tell you what will happen to you in days to come. 2 Assemble and hear, O sons of Jacob; listen to Israel your father.

8 'Judah, your brothers shall praise you;
your hand shall be on the neck of your enemies;
your father's sons shall bow down before you.

9 Judah is a lion's whelp;
from the prey, my son, you have gone up.
He crouches down, he stretches out like a lion,
like a lioness — who dares rouse him up?

10 The sceptre shall not depart from Judah,
nor the ruler's staff from between his feet,
until tribute comes to him;
and the obedience of the peoples is his.

11 Binding his foal to the vine
and his donkey's colt to the choice vine,
he washes his garments in wine
and his robe in the blood of grapes;

12 his eyes are darker than wine,
and his teeth whiter than milk.

'Judah' refers to Passion, Desire and Lust. These three traits rule every flesh without any exception in this physical world. Verse 8 names the three in order and with acceleration in degree. When it is in the state of passion, everyone praises it, when it accelerates to lust after it gains power through passion and desire, it won't let go but rockets to lust in the case of individual with authority, at this stage people will bow down to it. Verse 9, desire can go up and down depending on situations, but it has been fed on 'prey', the object of the desire, passion and lust. Verse10, individuals in authority and their sensual pleasure do not separate from the three till they are satisfied. And all people follow their own desires, passions and lust. Verse11 he ties his new desire to a business, fix his matured business to the chosen one, and wrapped them in attractive cover or package. Verse12, the desire makes his eyes red, the words used to describe the business are so 'pure'.

Look at today's world and see what's going on in every aspect of life on Earth, and read the verses again quietly by yourself. I know what your feelings are, just let them out if you want to cry!

Simeon and Levi – anger and wrath

5 'Simeon and Levi are brothers;
   weapons of violence are their swords.
6 May I never come into their council;
   may I not be joined to their company -
   for in their anger they killed men,
   and at their whim they hamstrung oxen.
7 Cursed be their anger, for it is fierce,
   and their wrath, for it is cruel!
   I will divide them in Jacob,

and scatter them in Israel.

Reuben, Simeon, Levi and Judah were all born to Leah, and in a succession, but the scripture put Simeon and Levi together and again emphasizes that 'they are brothers', because it is required so, for 'anger and wrath' are closely related traits, and anger can easily accelerate to wrath. Verse 5-6 Anger and wrath are the triggers of violence which becomes swords that will bring killings of men, and animals just for a moment of pleasure. Verse 7 Spirit never advises them nor joins them. They will not thrive or be welcome because they are fierce and cruel. (likely) People with anger and wrath will be divided at beginning, separated at later stage

Therefore it buried a clue for one of Jesus' sayings in Gospel of Thomas:

"A grapevine has been planted outside of the Father, but being unsound, it will be pulled up by its roots and destroyed."

This saying refers to Moses, because Moses was born from the offspring of Levi (wrath), who conceived him in Egypt. Moses was born and grown up in Egypt which is away from their Father's land and he played wrath on Egyptians while he was trying to take his people out of Egypt. This will be elaborated in part two of this writing.

Why does this grape vine has to be pulled out and destroyed?

As it was already revealed in previous session, from Abraham, to Issac, to Jacob (Israel) they were following a demigod led by their own strong desires, a single Yang energy manifestation, of which they were not aware of course, therefore they 'being unsound'. Historians cannot find any evidence about any equivalence on Israel tribes in related historical times except one line in an inscription about the name 'Israel' dated 1209 BCE, of the Egyptian pharaoh Merneptah. The inscription is very brief and says simply: "Israel is laid waste and his seed is not". And all available information today about the twelve tribes of Israel seems originated from Biblical scriptures. This is another proof to the revelation above – 'Israel' was same as his father, grandfather, being seeded, not grow, but wasted.

In linking to today's world, look at Judah, the lion – passion, desire and lust, has prevailed in every corner of the world, every aspect of social and individual life. And this has fulfilled another Jesus' saying that was mentioned before in this book:

Jesus said, *"Blessed is the lion which becomes man when consumed by man; and cursed is the man whom the lion consumes, and the lion becomes man."*

All other traits are related to individuals, but Judah, the lion is recognized as influencing and prevailing in the entire social economic structures - the money-driven scheme.

This money-driven scheme has been running in human society for thousands of years, no doubt it has contributed to the development of the society till modern days. As all things come and go in evolution, the money-driven scheme has finished its historical mission and it already becomes a big hinder for further social advancement as demonstrated by all the social issues humanity are facing now, therefore it needs to be banished sooner or later. If the main players in the society do not take actions gradually and peacefully, then the nature would cause it happen, by then it may be too late. Most of you probably agree that everything existing has its reason and everything has its timing. It is time that money-driven scheme and currency in the society to start moving out from your sight, and this is the calling from the Heaven and Earth!

When you observe the society, nature has already taken its course: more basic barter trading have already come back to the society in recent years, and coupons have been in use in some business, however they are still closely tied to the profit-driven scheme which needs to be guided and changed gradually. And virtual currencies appeared in the last couple of years which also needs to be clearly directed.

As many of you may have already identified it is the social structure that caused the problems in human society, as the current pope said in his new document Evangelii Gaudium "As long as the problems of the poor are not radically resolved by rejecting the absolute autonomy of markets and financial speculation and **by 'attacking' the structural causes of inequality**, no solution will be found for the world's problems or, for that matter, to any problems".

It is not just the problems of the poor, it is the survival of human species and all other living beings on Earth which is threatened because of the fundamentally out-of-date human social structures and belief systems. However it is not radical but natural to replace out-of-date social schemes with natural fits.

It is time for everyone who cares about the survival of human species, the wellbeing of yourself and your kindred and all living beings on Earth to take actions!

Urgent Call for Actions to Individuals, Organizations and Governments

A. Reduce human population by about 1/3 in 20 years peacefully; reduce human activity by 50% in 3-5 years

B. Take actions and steps to remove currency in social scheme within 20 years and encourage barter trading without using any form of currency, instead virtual scores for accounting purpose and goodness credit building

C. Religion reforms

Details:

1. Individuals and organizations are called for voluntarily donating 50% income to fund on the three kinds of projects:
   - Human population control and management projects. It may need to have an international accord, enforcement by each nation
   - Human soul salvation, spiritual awakening projects

- Green projects for restoration of nature. Returning natural habitats to wild animals and wildlife rehabilitation projects

2.   United Nations and national governments take actions on vigorous population control with international plans and national plans:
- The world calls on urgency for population control, taking actions to halt the growth of human population and reduce it worldwide, nationwide, and individually by 1/3 within 20 years; after that keep population growth and death rate roughly same
- Countries, like China, India etc. need to take further steps to control their population
- Reduce human activities by 50% in 3-5 years: you can consider half day working hours;
two meal diets; give time for individuals to be solitary; individuals assign time for meditation and exercise everyday to train both your Spiritual muscles and physical muscles to become a true well being, to ensure a healthy human species as a whole

3. Countries and regional territories take steps to gradually remove currencies within 20 years, encourage barter trading towards natural occurrences with whole scale multi-lateral participants. Virtual counting, virtual currency may be applied for accounting purposes only or simply use score for accounting purpose and goodness credit building, 'on demand and need' is the

principle of trading and production instead of profit and accumulation on material wealth

4. No more new shelters should be built for human beings except replacement, you have more than enough already; no shelters should be made with unsustainable materials from underground

5. Religion reforms. There is only One God, whatever you want to call it; there is only one Religion, the religion of Eternal Love; there is only one family, the Eternal Family of Humankind which is created in the image of God, with Yin and Yang energy in it. Also a larger Eternal Family with all other living beings as your cousins

    All religions are called and advised to take your respective reforms to recognize in your scriptures the core messages and guide people to know about the Oneness God and the Eternal Families and Eternal Love. Religion become one of the facilitators for human's soul wakening process besides other spiritual practices.

6. Individuals: Meditate, train yourself to fix your mind on the Oneness God, the Universal Supreme Consciousness; balance your time between doing and being, to live a peaceful and happy life. Return to nature, work on preparation for becoming a new body, embarking the journey to enter the Garden of Eden, the enlightened Kingdom.

The True Change Has Come!

Economists, scientists, environmentalists, visionaries, government officials, philanthropists, you need to form a fellowship to work out specific initiatives and plans for the focused tasks, and constitute new standards for all social activities

All earth citizens are called to participate in these reforms according to your new conscious standard.

Those 'clever' minds doing 'business', who may think you are on the front of a new wave of social movements and just apply some fashioned words in your daily deeds as in previous social waves, instead of completely shedding off the olds in every aspects of your life, I say to you, 'you are playing with fire!'

This is not a wave as you have experienced before that rose and fell away; this is a non-stop flood, soon it will form an ocean to cover the entire Earth. Those who cannot swim will get drawn even though you can board on a ship because there are storms on the ocean. It is wise that now you focus on learning the skills of swim before the flood turns into an ocean!

God Bless You!

Jesus Christ said:

"I took my place in the midst of the world, and I appeared to them in the flesh. I found all of them intoxicated; I found none of them thirsty. And My soul became afflicted for the sons of men, because they are blind in their hearts and do not have sight; for empty they came into the world, and empty too they seek to leave the world. But for the moment they are intoxicated. When they shake off their wine, then they will repent."

This was the world some two thousand years ago when Jesus first came; I hope you do not want to see Him pain again in his soul after some two thousand years, for at any minute He may return! And I see many of you have already shaken off your wine and start drinking from His mouth. You are blessed!

About the Authors

I am truly not keen to writing anything about me, it is irrelevant if you know me or not. The most important thing is the messages coming through me from The One Supreme Conscious Mind which you and I are part of, are surely heard. Just to satisfy the tendency of human's minds to know how the process of these messages take in shape, here are a little bit about where my flesh body was crystallized and how my individual mind is operating.

I was born in the midst of chaos in a place called Beijing when people there fought to each other. My family was sent to the bottom of the society because of my father's background with the kuomintang troops and his courage against injustice.

In my twenties, fate led me to step into a Christian church in Beijing. Tears rushed down my face the first day while I was sitting on the pews just by hearing the organ. Immediately I felt I found home. Soon I became a member of the choir, so enjoyed singing hymns almost everywhere and spread the gospels of God. Probably the next year I was baptized. I remember I was so pious in the spreading of God's news and even had some small miracles in my life. But later amidst a clerical election event on a Sunday when everybody went to the church to worship God, I picked up in the church yard a flyer on which there was a full story of denouncing languages sent by one of the candidates to the other. My heart was immediately tightened and my mind was confused. This and some other events happened later made me rethink about what the churches preached and gradually I stopped going to churches, and went on my journey to seek further. After I came to the United States I went to a couple of churches, of course similar, only added were a bit more commercial elements.

I believe there is a Divine force, I call it God, and I feel He is always with me. But my belief and understanding have already gone beyond what the churches have been preaching. In a quest of searching my soul mate and potential self-value, I become a student of Bhagavad Gita, the core part of a Hindu ancient epic, and have been pulled to study together horizontally with couple of other ancient texts. On the journey of the quest, I cannot stop asking so many questions, they just emerged to me naturally:

Questions I and other people asked:

1. There are so many religions and religion believers in the world who are followers of gods, deities and most of the religions want people to love, to respect, to help the poor, but what we see among them are cursers of peers using the most vicious languages to humiliate generations of their rivals in order to have a gain, we see demoralization in those priests who are supposed to be leading the

followers and we also see wars, massive destructions, poverty, whatever undesirable things keep rising among people all over the world. And most of the religions can be traced back to thousands of years. Why do these undesirable things still happen if the preaches can deliver salvation to you as claimed?

2. Since when there have always been wars and violent conflicts, conquers and rebellions that have been brought bloodsheds in humanity? And does it have to be this way?

3. How many times had a social movement or an influential event involved such a massive number of people who so piously and fervently threw themselves into it in the aim of liberating themselves and their brothers and sisters but in the end many of them felt cheated or taken advantage of and regretted forever? And instead only a few at the top 'achieved' their goal but after a while they became again the target of being removed? And why and how those a few people, one at a time, had the power to will the world or part of the world to achieve their 'agenda'?

4. Why is it that almost all the 'communist' countries in the world collapsed except that China is kept, to the surprise of many people in the world?

5. Nowadays almost all who live in the commercial world have the experience of being bombarded by sales information from different channels, and maybe more

than half of them on 50% price cut, and 99.99% of the sales information you wish not to receive at all. Perhaps no one likes this way in life, but in the end everyone does the same to anyone else. Why?

6. How come when two people have experienced exact the same events, pleasant or unpleasant, pleasure or hardship, but one of them emerges into a great leader who is the center of the world's admiration and respect, but the other becomes a violence adopter who bears the taste of bitterness?

7. One of the most commonly asked questions from other people - I know my father, or whoever it may be, is such a kind person, very religious, or I know my friend is a very kind and good person, how could he or she get cancer and die?

8. Ever with such a passion and faith in your dreams and oaths in a relationship, how come after a few years, some may make it longer, it all becomes an illusion, nothing can ignite the flame to arouse romance anymore? Have you ever dreamed of having a soul mate, and have you found it?

9. How many times in one moment you're enjoying the bliss and abundance that Law of Attraction has brought you and praise God for His Miracles, then another moment you are thrown into an abyss with a thread of 'bad' things happening, making you think you are really in

hell, and nobody can give you a hand. So what should you believe? etc. etc.

At the dawn of the new world order as the humanity transforms to a much uplifted society, I still see many powerful people and organizations doing business as usual with an attempt to exuberate much control and manipulation in order to bring in more profits which result in much destruction as a consequence, and so many talents, so much energy and resources are being wasted because of their ignorance about themselves and nature and their sense of losing directions. However the strong callings for a shift to an enlightened world, for a life of equality, justice and freedom I hear from everywhere in the world, I feel the power of Creation, I experience many tribes of beautiful souls with radiant lights.

A hero that has the courage to carry the burden to fulfill the quest is not a fairy elf, or Gandhalf the wizard or the to-be-king Aragon, but a little Hobbit who has no big desire from a little unknown place, because *"the magic power of the One Ring can easily consume the will of anyone and magnify the darkness of its Lord"*. Even Frodo toward the end could not resist its temptation, only with the help of Sam, and Gollum under the Providence of Divine, the One Ring has been destroyed in the Fire where it was originally forged. The Quest has been fulfilled. Truly 'This day does not belong to one man" and it cannot belong to one man because it has required a full range of qualities that belong to all men, plus the faith and efforts from all who have hope for a peaceful land.

This book was due long time ago because I felt it might stir adversity. However I would rather die if I did not take this assignment.

Also I was originally thinking of writing a 20,000 pocket manual book to facilitate the soul wakening process for the conscious shift of individuals; however after I started writing, more messages and information just kept being revealed to me, I was guided to access all the information needed. So the assignment has been completed as two parts of a writing with about 60,000 words. The world is calling for it! And God wants it to be unsealed now!

It is not about me. It is about you, about the world, about all other beings on Earth, in the universe! There probably some who have already seen what I see, however I am blessed with the courage and strength required.

Thank you God, it is You who gives me the courage, strength; it is You who bestowed upon me with wisdom, and moment by moment You stay by side of me! I know You are always with me! May Glory Be Yours! Amen!

If I have to acknowledge anyone who came to the physical world, as any book authors do, it is my flesh father. It was him who gave me the name 'New Wisdom', and God leads me in living up to it. His name: DEPU 德普 and DAOHONG道弘, meaning '普天地之德，弘天地之道 Spreading the Virtue of Heaven and Earth, Preaching the

Law of Heaven and Earth'.

Do not seek me. For the sake of all, I am living in retreat.
My twin sister Helen Xinhui is a visionary, an educator, she
has the most beautiful and purest heart I have ever seen.
She is also my dearest friend. She can handle all matters
related to the book on behalf of me; I require her to live a
semi-retreat life. You too should live a semi retreat life if
you want to enter the Kingdom earlier. God Bless All!

I would like to end the introduction by the lines below:

I am not my name,

I am not my culture,

I am not my training;

I am simply I am.

Through meditation I stay within God

With prayers I converse with Spirit

Within God I have nothing to fear and

My Spirit grows day by day

In Source I shuttle between the two worlds,

In Love I see the beauty of all God's creations

In Peace I understand all living beings and the universe

In detachment I experience freedom

In gentleness I show strength

In gratitude I offer my service to God's will

In service I fulfill the mission for reunion with my

Soul Mate in heaven

I am simply I am

Eternal, Immortal, Universal, and Infinite!

X.H. New Wisdom

Notes: scriptures are based on the versions listed below

1. Bhgavad Gita As It Is   second edition by A. C. Bhaktivedanta Swami Prabhupada

2. The Gospel of Thomas
   - Coptic version (translation: Thomas O. Lambdin)
   - Greek fragments (translation: B.P Grenfell & A.S. Hunt Bentley Layton)

3. TaoTeJing, translation of quoted verses by X.H. New Wisdom

4. Genesis, Exodus, Deuteronomy
   - The New Revised Standard Version (Anglicized Edition) copyright 1989, 1995 by the Division of Christian Education of the National Council of the Churches of Christ in the United States of America. Used by permission. All rights reserved.

   - King James version

5. The Gospel of Matthew, The New Revised Standard Version (Anglicized Edition)

6. Other versions of Genesis:
   - New International Version
   - New Living Translation
   - English Standard Version
   - New American Standard Bible

Disclaimer

This book is written in the spirit of openness, aiming at placing an objective reflection on humanity, teaching and exploring the science of God, Spirit and Consciousness of human beings; it does not intend to serve the interests of any particular religious or political groups. The authors believe that spiritual leaders work for the wellbeing of all living beings in existence instead of the interests of particular groups.

Other Learn With Universal Mind Books

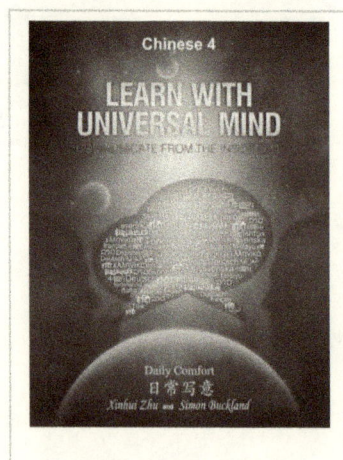

Other Learn With Universal Mind Books